America
Through the Lens

Martin W. Sandler

America
Through the Lens

Photographers Who Changed the Nation

HENRY HOLT AND COMPANY   NEW YORK

I am, as always, grateful for the help and support of my agent,
John Thornton. I also wish to thank Carol Sandler for her many
contributions. I am particularly indebted to Reka Simonsen—her
skill and guidance go well beyond her acknowledged editing skills
and shine through on every page.

Henry Holt and Company, LLC, *Publishers since 1866*
115 West 18th Street, New York, New York 10011
www.henryholt.com

Henry Holt is a registered trademark of Henry Holt and Company, LLC
Copyright © 2005 by Martin W. Sandler
All rights reserved. Distributed in Canada by H. B. Fenn and Company Ltd.

Library of Congress Cataloging-in-Publication Data
Sandler, Martin W.
    America through the lens: photographers who changed the nation / Martin W. Sandler.—1st ed.
        p.   cm.
    Includes bibliographical references and index.
    ISBN-13: 978-0-8050-7367-6
    ISBN-10: 0-8050-7367-1
    1. Photographers—United States. 2. Photography—United States. I. Title.

TR139.S25 2005   770'.92'273—dc22   2004059601

First Edition—2005 / Book designed by Meredith Pratt
Printed in China

10   9   8   7   6   5   4   3   2   1

This book is dedicated to all the men and women, amateur and professional, who have used their cameras to remind us of all that is good in our lives and all that needs to be corrected.

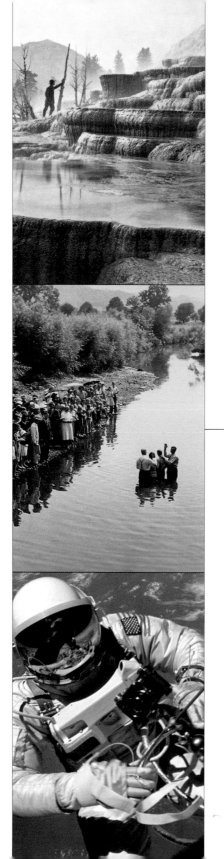

CONTENTS

For those of us accustomed to being surrounded by photographs, it is hard to imagine what a sensation they caused when they were introduced in 1839. For the first time people could have exact likenesses of themselves to give to friends and loved ones. People could also see what the celebrities of their day really looked like, individuals they had previously only read about.

As more efficient types of cameras were invented, photographers began to use them for purposes other than making portraits. Some took striking pictures of the landscape surrounding them and of places around the world that few people would ever have the chance to visit. Others captured images of important events as they were happening, changing forever the way the world received its news. Still other photographers took pictures whose sole purpose was to convey beauty, photographs that would earn their place in museums and galleries alongside paintings as true works of art. In modern times, such innovations as easy-to-use disposable cameras and instant and digital photography have combined to make taking pictures the most popular hobby the world has ever known.

INTRODUCTION

The camera has never been more important or far-reaching than when it has been in the hands of photographers who have dedicated themselves to bringing about change. From photography's earliest days, there have been cameramen and camerawomen who have been driven to, as photographer Lewis Hine so aptly put it, "show the things that need to be appreciated; show the things that need to be changed."

That is what this book is all about. In it you will meet men and women who, often against great odds, brought about needed change. You will, for example, encounter Mathew Brady, America's first prominent photographer, whose pictures dramatically changed the nation's attitude about war. You will meet Lewis Hine, who spent years of his life taking pictures of the millions of young children working from dawn to dusk in factories, canneries, and mines, pictures so powerful that they were instrumental in the abolishment of child labor. And you will be introduced to Frances Benjamin Johnston, whose photographs of African Americans in the post–Civil War years gave the world a portrayal of these people far different from any that had ever before been presented.

These are but three of the talented and dedicated people you will meet. All were highly skilled. Many of their pictures stand on their own as photographic masterpieces. But their true legacy is the way they brought about needed changes in attitudes and conditions, and in doing so helped make America, and the world in general, a better place in which to live. There can be no greater contribution.

—Martin W. Sandler
COTUIT, MASSACHUSETTS

America
Through the Lens

Mathew B. Brady

(1823–1896)

Changing the Way We View Our World

"A spirit in my feet said 'go,' and I went."

With that simple statement Mathew B. Brady explained why he had risked both his life and his fortune to give America a photographic record of the Civil War. Brady had already changed the way people viewed their world by becoming a pioneer in the field of photography. Soon he would change the nation's attitudes toward war.

Born in 1823 in Warren County, New York, Brady became fascinated with paintings as a child and decided he wanted to be an artist. An ambitious young man, he was able, at the age of sixteen, to gain an apprenticeship with the well-known painter William Page.

Mathew Brady said that "from the first, I regarded myself as under obligation to my country to preserve the faces of its historic men and mothers."

On a fateful day in 1839, Page introduced his apprentice to a fellow artist and friend, Samuel F. B. Morse. A professor of painting and design in New York, Morse was a man of many interests and had just completed his first invention. He called it the telegraph, and it would revolutionize the world of communications.

But Morse already had another new interest. He had recently returned from Paris where he had met with Louis Daguerre. The Frenchman had just astounded the prestigious French Academy by demonstrating his success in capturing permanent images through the lens of a camera, something that inventors and scientists had been trying to accomplish for hundreds of years. Daguerre had shown Morse how to produce such pictures, which he called daguerreotypes, and now Morse was starting a class in the astounding new process.

To Brady, daguerreotypes were miraculous. There before him was a picture of a person—not an interpretation drawn by an artist but an exact likeness of the individual. Young as he was, Brady realized that this new invention, which would come to be called photography, would change the world. He enrolled in Morse's class.

Brady quickly mastered techniques of the new daguerrotype process. He was so adept that he soon learned all that Morse could teach him. On his own, he began experimenting with ways to produce the most interesting pictures possible.

It was not easy. In those days people had to sit before the camera for as long as thirty minutes in order for an image to take. And they had to remain perfectly still. Head clamps were often used to keep subjects from moving. Because artificial lighting had not been perfected, the earliest daguerreotypes were taken outdoors in full sunlight. Many of those who sat for photographs came away with a sunburn and only a single image for their trouble, since daguerrotypes could not be reproduced.

Yet almost everyone felt that the painful experience was worth it. For the first time, people could have exact likenesses of themselves to share with their relatives and friends. And most could

Brady's New York City photographic gallery was a beehive of activity in which more than thirty thousand portraits were produced every year.

afford it. Unlike artists' portraits, which were so costly that only the wealthy could have them made, daguerreotypes were relatively inexpensive.

Soon there were daguerreotype studios in almost every city in the United States. Most of them were run by unskilled photographers who wanted only to earn a living from their work. But Mathew B. Brady took a different approach.

Rather than opening his own studio immediately, he spent almost five years perfecting his skills and reading everything that had been published on the new art. He consulted with scientists, seeking ways to improve the chemical aspects of the daguerreotype process. He took scores of pictures, experimenting with different types of poses and props that would allow him to create images that were far more appealing than those being turned out by most of the other early photographers. One of his major innovations was the introduction of a huge skylight as part of his

photographic setup, which made it possible to take pictures as effectively indoors as in full sunlight.

Finally, in 1844, at the age of twenty-four, Brady opened his own establishment. He rented rooms on the top floor of a building at the busy corner of Broadway and Tenth Street in New York City and announced he was ready for business. It was more than just a studio, for there was also a gallery where a large number of Brady's daguerreotypes were displayed.

Brady understood from the beginning that if he was to outdistance his competitors he could not go it alone; rather, he would need to put together the best team of camera operators, chemists, retouchers, colorists, and other assistants he could assemble. He took very few of the pictures himself, leaving that to the camera operators. Instead, he coordinated the talents of all his assistants and concentrated on the more creative aspects of setting up the pictures, particularly that of determining the most interesting angles from which the photographs were to be shot.

Brady's gallery caused a sensation. People flocked there to view the pictures on display and to have their likenesses recorded. Many famous political leaders and celebrities also came to have their pictures taken.

Buoyed by his success, Brady soon opened a second studio in Washington, D.C., where he would be even closer to the prominent political figures of his day. There he photographed every living president of the United States, from John Quincy Adams to William McKinley.

Unquestionably the most important person Brady photographed was Abraham Lincoln. He took his first picture of Lincoln

Thousands of copies of Brady's Cooper Union portrait of Abraham Lincoln were sold throughout the nation, and drawings made from the image were published in leading newspapers of the day.

The pictures taken by Brady's corps of Civil War cameramen, including those of the various troops drilling between battles, marked the beginning of American military photography.

during the 1860 presidential campaign, a time when the tall, gangly candidate was unknown to most Americans and was commonly portrayed as an ugly country bumpkin by cartoonists who supported his opponent. Brady photographed the future president just before he delivered an important speech at Cooper Union in New York. Aware of the importance of the picture, Brady used all his skills to produce an image that would present the candidate in the most appealing, dignified manner possible.

By this time, Brady had learned a brand-new photographic process, one that used a glass wet-plate negative. It was coated with a sticky substance, which meant that it had to be developed as soon as the picture was taken, before the substance dried. Although it had this drawback, it had a major advantage over the daguerreotype process: Many copies of a particular photograph could be reproduced from a wet-plate negative.

Delighted with the result of the portrait Brady had made, Lincoln had his campaign workers distribute the photograph throughout the country. When Lincoln won the election, he publicly declared that "Brady and the Cooper Union speech made me president." Brady took many of the best-known photos of Lincoln, including the one used as the model for the Lincoln penny.

If Mathew B. Brady had never taken another picture after 1860, he still would have gone down in history as a photography giant, the man who gave Americans a new way of viewing their world. But in 1861 the Civil War erupted into the most tragic conflict in the history of the United States.

Brady made an important decision. He would travel to the Civil War camps and battlefields and give the nation a photographic record of the war. With President Lincoln's permission, Brady organized a team of more than twenty

Although the cameras of their day could not record movement, Brady's photographers were able to depict the devastating nature of the war by showing weapons that were far more destructive than any previously used in combat.

photographers to help him. He supplied the team with a huge array of cameras, chemicals, and other equipment, and with horsedrawn wagons to carry the gear.

Brady and his photography corps captured thousands of images of soldiers as they relaxed in camp, drilled during periods between battles, and operated some of the largest weapons the world had ever known. Field hospitals, long lines of supply wagons, acres of piled-up munitions, military trains, hastily erected bridges, telegraph corpsmen, nurses and doctors— everything that had to do with the war was photographed. Mathew Brady and his team were the first photographers to record a major event in the nation's history.

The Civil War photographs dramatically disclosed how young many of the combatants on both sides were. This fourteen-year-old Confederate private was killed in battle shortly after Brady took his picture.

However, the most telling of all the images were those of the thousands from both armies who lay dead and dying on the battlefields. When the war had begun, the North and the South had each believed that it would be a brief conflict. Many had cheered on their departing troops as if they were embarking upon a great adventure. Brady and his photographers changed all that. Their haunting pictures disclosed the incredible price in human lives paid by both sides.

Photos of dead Union and Confederate soldiers lying side by side did more to shock Americans into an awareness of the horrors of war than words could ever have accomplished.

The photos were sent straight from the battlefields to be displayed in Brady's studios, where they made the horror of war inescapable. The nation was shocked. "Mr. Brady," stated one newspaper, "has done something to bring home to us the terrible reality and earnestness of war." Thanks to Mathew B. Brady, Americans would never look at war in the same way again.

Brady and his photographers gave the nation an unforgettable portrait of the physical destruction brought about by war, as this picture of once-beautiful Richmond, Virginia, clearly shows.

William Henry Jackson

(1843–1942)

Preserving Our Natural Treasures

"He was one of the most important figures of the late nineteenth century."

That is how noted historian Edwin Rozwenc described the accomplishments of William Henry Jackson. Born in Kesseville, New York, in 1843, Jackson began his career as an apprentice photographer. He was only fifteen, and photography itself was less than twenty years old.

When the Civil War broke out in 1861, Jackson joined the Union army and spent the next three years drawing maps and sketching enemy campsites for his unit. When he left the service in 1863, he went to work

"Portrait photography," stated William Henry Jackson, "never had any charms for me, so I sought out subjects from the house-tops and finally from the mountain tops. . . ."

in a photographic studio in Burlington, Vermont. Three years later, brokenhearted after his engagement to a young woman fell apart, the always restless Jackson decided to change his life completely by trying his luck in the West.

For the next two years he drifted from place to place and from job to job in the still vastly unsettled western territories. He worked first as a guard on a wagon train,

15

then as a carpenter and farmhand, and finally as an art tutor. In 1868, tired of drifting, Jackson finally settled down in Omaha, Nebraska, where he opened his own photography studio.

It was an exciting time in Nebraska. The Union Pacific, one of two companies involved in building the nation's first transcontinental railroad, was laying hundreds of miles of track through the territory. Anxious to document its progress, the company hired Jackson to photograph the tracklayers and other workers, the trains, and all the activities that were part of the most difficult and ambitious construction project that had ever been undertaken in America. For more than a year, Jackson followed the building of the railroad with his camera, producing pictures that impressed all who saw them.

One of those who was particularly taken with the photographs was Ferdinand V. Hayden, an accomplished scientist. Hayden had been appointed the leader of a government expedition formed to survey, map, and provide geological information about vast areas of the West that were still largely unknown to most U.S. citizens. His task was to lead his expedition into Wyoming's Yellowstone region, one of the most rugged and unexplored areas of the western territories. After seeing the railroad pictures, Hayden asked Jackson to join his team as the expedition's official photographer. Jackson's acceptance of that position was the turning point in his life and career.

In 1871 the Hayden party entered the region named for the Yellowstone River that flowed through it, aware that very few people other than Native Americans had ever set foot there. Those early explorers who had been in the area told amazing

As one photography critic noted, Jackson's images of the Yellowstone region "helped transform perceptions of the West from a mythical realm to a place that could actually be visited and settled."

stories of majestic, snowcapped mountains from which flowed enormous waterfalls that cascaded thousands of feet to the earth below. Within these mountains, said eyewitnesses, were hundreds of canyons containing bizarre rock formations.

Even more astounding were the tales of scores of natural geysers that sent fountains of water exploding high into the air. There were also reports of dozens of springs in which boiling water bubbled continuously. The stories were entertaining, but few who heard them believed that they were true. At best they had to be wild exaggerations. But Hayden and his team quickly discovered the stories were not false. They weren't exaggerated. As the men ventured deeper into the area and looked around them, they realized that, if anything, the early descriptions had been understated. For Jackson, in particular, the first encounter with the wonders of Yellowstone was an emotional experience. He understood that seeing these marvels was one thing; photographing them in a way that did justice to their splendor was something else again.

While photography had come a long way since Mathew Brady had introduced the medium to America, taking a picture was still a difficult task. The cameras were large and bulky. In order to keep them perfectly still while capturing an image, a photographer had to mount them on a tripod. Even more demanding was the process of preparing and developing the large glass negatives the cameras used.

Like all photographers of his day, Jackson had to prepare each of his negatives himself by pouring a sticky, light-sensitive chemical solution over them. These so-called wet plates had to be used quickly and then developed within minutes after the picture was taken or they would dry out and the picture would be ruined. This

In order to do justice to subjects once seen only by Native Americans, Jackson chose to take many of his Yellowstone photographs at an angle that would best reveal the size and grandeur of the place.

made picture-taking difficult under any circumstances. Preparing a plate, taking a picture, and then developing it on the spot in a vast, rugged area such as Yellowstone was challenging almost beyond belief.

As he traveled throughout the region, Jackson carried with him three cameras, several tripods, boxes of chemicals, and a portable developing tent. Heaviest of all the equipment were the huge glass negatives, which were sixteen by twenty inches. Like all his materials, they were transported on the back of a mule and hauled up and down mountains, across the floors of deep canyons, and throughout the areas where the geysers, hot springs, and other natural wonders were located.

Jackson was a tireless worker who spent several hours each day scouting for the scene he wished to photograph, setting up his equipment, and preparing his negatives. He was also a perfectionist. Even when perched precariously on a ledge jutting out from the top of a mountain, he waited patiently for just the right light to capture the image he sought. Most of the time he was rewarded with the masterful photograph he hoped for. Other times the weather deteriorated to such an extent that, after waiting for so long, he was unable to take even one picture. There were disasters as well. More than once a mule carrying glass plates slipped on the treacherous terrain as Jackson and the animal made their way back down the mountain. Jackson would watch in horror as the plates came loose from the straps that held them and shattered into pieces.

But he would not allow himself to be discouraged. He took hundreds of photographs that were remarkable not only for their rich variety and awe-inspiring content, but for their artistic quality. Fortunately for Jackson, he was not the only artist on the expedition. Hayden's team also included Thomas Moran, one of the nation's most accomplished landscape painters. Jackson and Moran quickly became friends, and soon they were helping each other in their work.

Moran provided Jackson with insights about how best to compose his photographs and helped him find the best spots from which to take his pictures. In turn, Jackson provided Moran with photographs that the artist used as the basis for many of the oil paintings that he did of the region.

Preparing the huge glass plates, packing and transporting them up a mountain on a mule, and waiting for the right moment to take a picture was a time-consuming process. The team often spent as many as four hours taking a single photograph.

Thanks to his own abilities, Moran's help, and his willingness to persist through trial and error, Jackson discovered the most effective ways of capturing the natural wonders that few had ever seen, and established himself as a master of the still-infant art of landscape photography. In the process he provided the documentary evidence that what had long been dismissed as wild rumors about Yellowstone were really true.

By the beginning of 1872 the members of the Yellowstone expedition had completed their official work, but as far as Ferdinand Hayden was concerned, another vital task lay directly ahead. From the first moment he had set foot in the region, he had been convinced that this was an area that had to be preserved in its natural state forever. His goal was to persuade Congress to pass a bill establishing Yellowstone as the country's first national park.

Hayden pursued this goal with the same determination that Jackson had displayed in taking his pictures. First he set up an exhibition of Jackson's photographs and Moran's paintings in the Capitol building, where members of Congress would be sure to see them. Then he showed some of Jackson's most dramatic pictures to individual legislators. Faced with such overwhelming visual evidence of Yellowstone's natural splendor, Congress was easily persuaded to act on Hayden's proposal. A bill making Yellowstone the first national park was introduced and passed with little opposition. On March 1, 1872, it was signed into law. Commenting on the historic event, Army Corps of Engineers Captain Hiram M. Chittenden wrote that Jackson's photographs "did a work that no other agency could do, and doubtless convinced everyone who saw them that the regions where such wonders existed should be preserved [for] the people forever."

The publicity that Jackson received as a result of his Yellowstone depictions led to the widespread publication of his photographs of the region and earned him a reputation as the foremost western photographer in the nation. Anxious to maintain

Capturing Yellowstone's geothermal wonders, such as the region's Mammoth Hot Springs, was a great challenge, but Jackson's skill and patience resulted in some of the most compelling landscape photographs ever taken.

THE ROCKY MOUNTAINS
SCENES ALONG THE LINE OF THE
DENVER AND RIO GRANDE RAILWAY.

Until Jackson took his now-famous picture of the Mount of the Holy Cross, it was a place that most people thought existed only in legend.

his services, the government hired him to be the official photographer for other geological surveys in the West and Southwest. For the better part of the next seven years, he took pictures that, in the words of one writer, "revealed the essential qualities of the West and reproduced the experience of contact with wilderness and God for millions of viewers." Some of these photographs, taken in such areas as Yosemite and the Grand Teton mountain range, contributed to these regions also eventually being established as national parks.

252

Jackson's photograph of the majestic Yellowstone Canyon was one of the key pictures used to persuade Congress to establish the region as the country's first national park.

It was while taking these later survey pictures that Jackson made yet another photographic breakthrough. In 1875 he packed a camera equipped to hold plates measuring twenty by twenty-four inches on the back of a mule and hauled them up the Rocky Mountains. "These are the largest plates ever used in field photography," Jackson wrote. "They convey an impression of the real grandeur and the magnitude of mountain scenery that the smaller views cannot possibly impart."

The images that Jackson was able to capture with his mammoth plates astounded the photographic world and provided Americans with an even greater portrayal of the wonders of the West. No other photographer had so visibly changed America.

That he was responsible, in considerable measure, for the beginnings of the national parks system cannot be questioned, but his contributions went much deeper. For it was William Henry Jackson who, through his photographs, helped alter many people's notion of the West from assuming that the place existed only in myth and fantasy to recognizing that it was real—and a national treasure.

William Henry Jackson's long and distinguished career as a landscape photographer was honored when this beautiful lake in what is now Wyoming's Grand Teton National Park was named for him.

JACKSON LAKE

Frances Benjamin Johnston

(1864–1952)

Documenting a Rise from Slavery

"For the sake of money or anything else,"

This self-portrait, which Frances Benjamin Johnston took in 1896, was designed to tell the world that here was a woman determined to break down the social taboos of her day.

said Frances Benjamin Johnston, "I would not publish a photograph that fell below the standard I set for myself." Always a perfectionist, Johnston was an individual who loved to shock people. She lived at a time when there were many things that women were not supposed to do, and most people believed that a woman's place was in the home. But Johnston broke all the rules. She smoked, she drank beer, and she even wore skirts that scandalously revealed her ankles. She was also the nation's—and perhaps the world's—first female photojournalist and broke down many of the taboos about women's place in society. Most important of all, she used her camera to provide a portrait of African Americans that changed the way they were regarded.

Johnston was born in Grafton, West Virginia, in 1864 and spent her early years in Rochester, New York, and Washington, D.C. When she was in high school she became interested in art, and at the age of nineteen she went to Paris where she studied painting and drawing for two years.

When she returned home she got a job with a New York magazine, writing articles that she illustrated with drawings. Although she had never taken a picture,

she was one of the first illustrators to realize the role that photography could play in journalism. She was captivated by the way camera images were more realistic and far more immediate than artists' illustrations. She was convinced that photos presented the best means ever introduced of enabling people to witness newsworthy events and to be made aware of conditions that merited their attention. She became determined to learn how to take pictures so that she could capture the types of images that would illuminate the important issues of her era.

George Eastman, who had recently revolutionized photography with his invention of the Kodak camera, was a family friend. Johnston told him of her intentions. The inventor sent her one of his new cameras. She then enrolled in a photography course at the Smithsonian Institution and learned the basic techniques of picture-taking.

When the course was over, Johnston opened her own photography studio. She was related to the nation's First Lady, Mrs. Grover Cleveland, and she used this connection to gain access to the White House. There she took scores of pictures of the president, his family, and many other political leaders and well-known figures. But as her interest was still in journalistic photography, she soon grew tired of taking this kind of picture.

Then Johnston got her first break. In 1891 the publisher of *Demorest's Family Magazine* commissioned her to take photographs to accompany articles the magazine was preparing on the Kohinoor coal mine in Pennsylvania and Mammoth Cave in Kentucky. It was a difficult assignment, even for a much more experienced photographer. Others had attempted to capture images in these

Johnston, standing in the center of this photograph, in front of her early portable studio, began her career taking tintypes, inexpensive portraits printed on thin sheets of metal.

underground places, but the lighting conditions there were so poor that they found it impossible to take good pictures.

Johnston was determined to succeed. Even though she had been warned that it was a dangerous idea, she put together a container filled with highly flammable powder to take into the mine, hoping that when she lit the powder it would provide enough light for picture-taking. Her invention worked, and she was able to shoot the first successful photographs ever taken in a mine. She repeated the same procedure at Mammoth Cave and the results were just as rewarding.

The underground photographs launched Johnston's photojournalistic career. From the beginning she understood the odds she would have to overcome in choosing a profession totally controlled by men, and she felt a responsibility to encourage other women to enter the world of photography. In 1897 Johnston published an article in the *Ladies' Home Journal* titled "What a Woman Can Do with a Camera." The article told women how to become a photographer, what training was involved, and how to establish and run a studio. "The woman who makes photography profitable," she wrote, must have "good common sense, unlimited patience to carry her through endless failures, equally unlimited tact, good taste, a quick eye, a talent for detail and a genius for hard work."

Johnston followed up her article in dramatic fashion. She collected 148 photographs taken by twenty-eight talented amateur American female photographers and arranged for them to be shown at exhibitions in Russia and Paris. The pictures were well received, and Johnston earned high praise for providing such convincing evidence of what women photographers could accomplish.

Johnston had a highly developed sense of composition, as can be seen in this photograph of a Hampton science class.

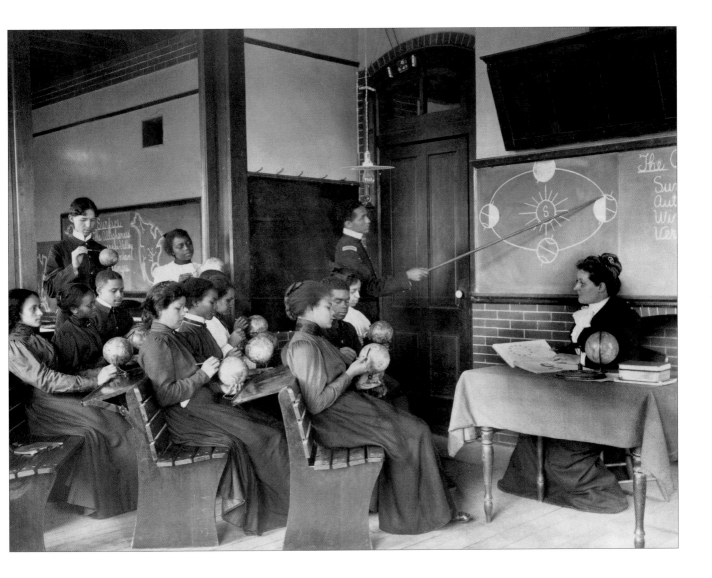

Then in 1899 Johnston received a commission to produce a series of photographs of the Washington, D.C., schools. The pictures were to be used in a series of small books describing the many facets of America's then-unique free public-school system.

The commission Johnston received called for her to take at least three hundred fifty photographs of the schoolchildren in various classes, on field trips, and involved in other activities. She was then to produce prints of all the pictures she took. Included also was a backbreaking deadline: She had to complete all of the work in six weeks.

Johnston not only fulfilled the requirements, she exceeded them. In under six weeks she took seven hundred striking photographs, images that not only brilliantly documented the school activities but revealed her photographic style.

When the school pictures were completed, they were taken to Europe, where they were shown at the prestigious Paris Exposition of 1900. They were an enormous hit, earning Johnston the exhibition's grand prize for photography. She had scored a triumph, but, even though she could not have known it at the time, her most important work still lay ahead.

The success of Johnston's Washington school pictures led other institutions to seek out her talents. Among them was a request from General Samuel Chapman Armstrong, the founder of Hampton Institute in Virginia. Hampton had been established for the purpose of taking uneducated young African Americans, only recently freed from slavery, and training them in skilled labor. Hampton students were taught to be carpenters, cobblers, milliners, cooks, and tradespeople of all kinds. In a time of

Johnston's Hampton Institute photographs, like this one of carpentry students at work, often emphasized the school's main approach of "learning by doing."

bitter and widespread racism, lynchings, and severely limited opportunities for African Americans, the skills taught at Hampton offered black students their best chance of working their way out of poverty and building productive lives.

Johnston was aware of the importance of the project. She had long been outraged that many writers, artists, cartoonists, and theater shows had portrayed African Americans as shiftless and unintelligent. Furthermore, she knew that even among white Americans who were not actively racist the majority were still indifferent to the plight of blacks. For Johnston, the assignment was an opportunity to break new ground in the long struggle for African Americans to be recognized as a vital part of society.

Johnston took more than one hundred fifty photographs at Hampton Institute. They were, as one photography critic proclaimed, "images of stunning clarity and intensity." With each day she spent there, Johnston became more impressed with the students' devotion to their studies, their ability to grasp the skills they were being taught, and their appreciation of the opportunities they were being given.

As she had in her Washington school pictures, Johnston composed each photograph beautifully, making every picture a compelling image as well as a vital document. Most important of all was the way she was able to capture the students' earnest and dignified approach to their studies. She had come to Hampton hoping to help break down long-held racial stereotypes, and she did her job masterfully. Soon after the pictures were taken, they were published in several magazines, most notably *The American Monthly Review of Reviews*, and featured in several photographic exhibitions. Her work moved everyone who saw it, and prompted one critic

The photographs Johnston took of impoverished African Americans in the Deep South were, like her Hampton pictures, marked by the respectful way in which she preserved the dignity of all her subjects.

to write, "[The Hampton photographs] radiate such innocence and good hope that they make me want to cry."

When her work at Hampton was completed, Johnston traveled throughout the Virginia countryside taking photographs of black families, which were remarkable for capturing the dignity these people maintained despite their poverty. She also took pictures in the homes and small businesses of Hampton graduates who lived in

The teacher in the center of this photograph of a laboratory class at Tuskegee Institute was George Washington Carver, destined to become one of America's most innovative and respected scientists.

the area. The pictures revealed how the skills they had learned at Hampton Institute had helped them achieve success.

Just as Johnston was taking the last of her Virginia-countryside photographs, she received another important request. It came from Booker T. Washington, the most famous African American of his time. Washington, who had been schooled at

Johnston's portraits of successful black families in which a husband or a wife had graduated from Hampton Institute were used to publicize the value of a Hampton education.

Hampton, had gone on to become one of the nation's leading educators and, in 1881, had founded Tuskegee Institute in Alabama. Like Hampton, Tuskegee was established to provide young African Americans with an industrial education. Washington's larger purpose in founding the school was to use it as a model so that other "Tuskegees" could be established throughout the South.

Highly impressed by what her Hampton pictures had accomplished, Washington asked Johnston to come to Tuskegee to take a similar series of photographs. Johnston took her Tuskegee pictures in 1902. In August 1903, many of them were used to accompany an important article written by Washington, titled "The Successful Training of the Negro." In the article, Washington stressed the role of Tuskegee as a model for other schools. Later, when such schools were established, Washington publicly credited Johnston with having helped him and his fellow black educators attain their goal.

Frances Benjamin Johnston was a woman far ahead of her time. She showed women what could be done and then helped them do it. She showed the nation that many of its perceptions about its African-American citizens were outrageously false. And she did it all by setting her own standards and following her own rules. Irreverent to the end, she summed up her life with a simple statement: "I've learned not to depend on the Lord," she proclaimed. "I'll make the changes myself."

"She composed a portrait that evoked a true and lasting visual suggestion of the age," wrote a photography critic of Johnston's accomplishments.

Jacob Riis

(1849–1914)

Cleaning Up the Slums

"People have a right to lives with dignity and respect."

By applying this conviction to his picture-taking, Jacob Riis inspired reform and changed the lives of tens of thousands of newcomers to America.

Riis was himself an immigrant. In 1870 he had come from Denmark to the United States seeking to earn money to help

As a noted photography historian has stated, Jacob Riis, shown here taking pictures of immigrants in their tenement neighborhood, "revolutionized the way America looked at itself."

support his parents and his fourteen brothers and sisters back home. He had another reason for immigrating as well: He had fallen in love with a girl from his hometown, but her father forbade her to marry him until he had enough money to support her in comfort.

So Riis came to America, determined to make his fortune. Unwittingly he had arrived at a time when the nation was in the midst of a severe economic depression. He had almost no money and could find only odd jobs that paid very little. Sometimes he would wander the streets homeless. Often he would sleep on a bare mattress in the basement of one of the New York buildings called tenements in

which hundreds of newcomers lived huddled together in squalor. Several times he came close to starving.

Finally, in 1877, Riis's fortunes changed. He got a job as a police reporter for the *New York Tribune* and was soon able to pull himself out of poverty. But his years of sleeping in the tenements and observing the thousands who suffered there had affected him deeply. He had come to America to make his fortune, but now he had a very different goal. He would make the nation aware of the immigrants' desperate plight, hoping that somehow his words would bring about change.

He began by writing a series of articles for the *Tribune* describing the conditions that the immigrants, too poor to afford better housing, were forced to endure. The owners of the tenements were determined to make as much money as possible, so they packed as many people as they could inside the buildings. In the summers, hundreds of babies died from the sweltering heat because landlords had ignored building codes and put almost no windows in the tenements. The jam-packed structures, with their wooden stairways, wooden ceilings, and wooden floors, were firetraps, terrible disasters waiting to happen.

Riis's articles became a main feature of the *Tribune*, but, as far as he was concerned, they did not grab anywhere near the amount of attention they deserved. Frustrated by how little change his work for the *Tribune* had produced, Riis moved on to a more aggressive newspaper, the *New York Evening Sun*. He also began writing a book

Riis's pictures, such as this one of tenement dwellers in an alley between buildings, shocked most Americans and eventually earned him the title "emancipator of the slums."

that would more fully describe the conditions he was finding in his daily trips to the tenements. Most important, he came up with a bold, new approach. Aware that his words were not bringing the reactions he sought, he decided to begin taking photographs that would accompany his writing.

People might not be moved by his words or even believe what he wrote, but surely they would not be able to deny the shocking evidence that his pictures would provide.

It was an inspired idea, but Riis knew it presented two problems. First, he had almost no experience with a camera. Second, he was aware that in order to most effectively depict tenement conditions he would have to take most of his pictures in dark or dim rooms and hallways, and the cameras of the day were not able to take pictures in poorly lit places.

He solved the first problem on the job by taking photograph after photograph, improving his skills with each series of images. The second problem was solved for him. Just as Riis was forming his picture-taking plans, he read an article about a new photographic invention called a magnesium flash. It contained highly flammable powder that, when lit, created a flash of light bright enough to illuminate even the darkest place long enough for a picture to be taken.

The new magnesium flash was a marked improvement over the device Frances Benjamin Johnston had put together to make her coal-mine pictures. Riis immediately purchased one of the new flashes and, armed with it and a camera, resumed his trips to the slums. Some of the photographs he took were of the decrepit buildings themselves. Later, describing one of these pictures, he wrote, "These buildings, like the people living in them, have endured something awful."

He was right, but it was inside the tenements that he took his most dramatic and telling photographs. In a caption accompanying a picture he titled "Lodgers in a Bayard Street Tenement," he wrote, "In a room not thirteen feet

Many of Riis's photographs chronicle noble attempts to achieve some kind of civilized life. This portrait shows a Jewish cobbler determined to carry on his traditional Sabbath dinner in the squalid coal cellar in which he lived.

either way slept twelve men and women, two or three in bunks set up in a sort of alcove, the rest on the floor. A kerosene lamp burnt dimly in the fearful atmosphere, probably to guide later arrivals to their bed, for it was just after midnight."

One of the worst tenement areas was a section called Mulberry Bend. Here immigrants lived in damp basements, leaky attics, outhouses, and horse stables converted into dwellings. It was not uncommon for as many as forty families to live in just three or four of the tenement buildings there.

Riis's Mulberry Bend pictures captured the desperate expressions on the faces of the adults, the pathetic condition of the children, and the litter piled up in the dark alleys between the buildings. Riis also trained his camera on that area of "the Bend" known as Bandit's Roost, notorious for the many criminals who lived there. Riis photographed them standing in the alleys, perched on windowsills, and huddled underneath tenement porches.

Of all the horrors that Riis encountered he was most concerned with the plight of the children. He was outraged at the number who died each year because of the cold, damp, unhealthy rooms in which they lived. "Life in the tenements in July and August spells death to an army of little ones whom the doctor's skill is powerless to save," Riis wrote. "Here is a door. Listen! That short hacking cough, that tiny helpless wail [tells us that] the child is dying with measles. With half a chance it might have lived; but it had none. That dark bedroom killed it."

In this photograph Riis provided visual evidence of another evil of the tenement neighborhoods: the way in which downtrodden areas attracted bandits and other criminal types.

These were sounds that Riis could never forget, but they were also sounds that motivated him to work even harder. It was not only difficult work; it was dangerous as well. On more than one occasion he literally had to flee for his life from slum dwellers who

either did not understand why he was taking their picture or did not want to be photographed in such miserable surroundings.

He refused to be discouraged. And despite such abuses, he was careful not to demean any of his subjects. Many of his photographs document the noble attempt of people struggling against immense odds to achieve some kind of civilized life amid the squalor around them.

During the late 1870s, when Riis's articles were appearing regularly in the *Tribune*, and most of the 1880s, when he was a regular contributor to the *Evening Sun*, the techniques for printing photographs in newspapers, magazines, and books had not yet been perfected. The articles were illustrated with drawings copied from Riis's photographs. By 1889, however, the year in which he completed his book on the slums, a process had been invented that permitted photographs to be published alongside words on the printed page.

Riis called his book *How the Other Half Lives*. In 1889 sections of it appeared in *Scribner's*, one of the nation's most popular magazines. Then, in 1890, the book was published. It contained both actual photographs and drawings made from Riis's pictures. The country was stunned. People found it almost impossible to believe that so many were living under such horrendous conditions. One of those most shocked by the pictures was New York City's police commissioner, Theodore Roosevelt, who would later become president of the United States. Deeply touched by Riis's work, Roosevelt sent him a note saying, "I have read your book and I have come to help."

Roosevelt then began accompanying Riis on his rounds of tenements, alleys, and streets. Moved even more by what he saw firsthand,

Riis's honest portrayal of the plight of immigrants, particularly children, earned him high praise from fellow photographers and government officials alike.

The many reforms that were brought about by Riis's articles and photographs included the construction of playgrounds throughout the tenement districts.

Roosevelt got other top-ranking officials from New York and the federal government to read Riis's book and to visit the slums in person. Devastated by what they saw, the officials then spearheaded efforts to clean up the tenement neighborhoods.

But Riis's work was still not done. He spent the next twenty-five years writing articles and giving talks around the nation. He wrote over a dozen more books with

First as governor of New York and later as president of the United States, Theodore Roosevelt offered Jacob Riis several government positions, but Riis politely refused them all, stating that his work on behalf of the tenement dwellers was too important to abandon.

titles such as *Children of the Tenements*, *Out of Mulberry Street*, and *Children of the Poor*. Thanks in great measure to all he had done, genuine reform took place. Much of the slum district of New York City's Lower East Side was torn down. New, strict building codes and housing laws were passed to ensure that the buildings that replaced the tenements were cleaner and safer. Special places called settlement houses were established, where immigrants could learn to speak English and could acquire the skills needed to get decent jobs.

As conditions began to improve, Riis trained his camera on the progress that was being made. He took many pictures showing immigrant children receiving the benefits of America's public-school system, where they were able to acquire the knowledge that would enable them to build better lives than their parents had known.

Riis also took pictures of a project that was particularly close to his heart. He had always advocated replacing many of the tenements with parks that would bring fresh air and recreation into the lives of the immigrants. One of his greatest joys was that he lived long enough to see the infamous Mulberry Bend section replaced by a park named in his honor. Soon other parks would be built, and Riis would be further honored by becoming known as the founder of the small-parks movement.

By the time he died in 1914 at the age of sixty-five, Jacob Riis, through his photographs, had changed the lives of countless people and had even brought physical change to the nation's largest city. His contributions were so great that Theodore Roosevelt publicly called him "America's most useful citizen." Yet, ironically, Riis never thought of himself as a photographer. He continually stated that his only goal in taking pictures was to prove that what he was writing about was true.

Jacob Riis's leading role in fostering the replacement of tenement buildings with small parks was yet another major accomplishment of a man whose photographs have been described as "containing qualities which will last as long as man is concerned with his brother."

Lewis Hine

(1874–1940)

Letting Children Be Children

"If I could tell the story in words, I wouldn't need to lug around a camera."

Lewis Hine is widely regarded as the first photographer who used his work to bring about legislative change.

For more than forty-five years Lewis Hine hauled photographic equipment throughout the United States. The pictures he took were so powerful and moving that, like those of Jacob Riis, they became among the first photographs ever used to bring about needed changes in the nation's laws.

Lewis Hine was born in Oshkosh, Wisconsin, in 1874. He was introduced to photography in 1901 when the principal of the school in New York in which he was teaching asked him to take pictures that could be used as classroom aids. He had little experience with cameras, but he soon fell in love with photography. As part of his new assignment, Hine began taking his students out into the countryside to photograph nature. He also took them on photography trips throughout New York City. On one of these outings they went to the great immigration depot at Ellis Island, where millions of people from countries throughout Europe were pouring into America. Hine became fascinated with these men, women, and children who were risking everything to begin a new life in a new land.

Lewis Hine also took pictures of immigrants, but unlike Jacob Riis, whose photographs emphasized the horrors of immigrant tenement life, Hine's images, such as this one of a family waiting to leave their newly arrived ship, often focused on the newcomers' determination to succeed.

Hine began photographing the immigrants whenever he could. He took pictures of them gazing out from the decks of the newly arrived ships that had brought them on the long voyage across the Atlantic. He photographed them inside the Ellis Island facilities, where they had to withstand many physical and mental examinations before they were allowed to enter the country. He also took pictures in the crowded tenement buildings where most of the immigrants were forced to live.

Hine's photographs of the newcomers were different from most of the other portrayals of the time. Up to that point, many newspaper artists and cartoonists, suspicious of the hordes of immigrants with their "strange" clothing and languages, had depicted the recent arrivals as ignorant people lacking ambition. Hine knew this was not so. His photographs revealed the human side of the immigrants. In

Making artificial flowers was one type of work immigrants did in order to make a living. Many of Hine's early pictures documented the day-to-day work done by whole families in their new country.

their faces he captured the hopes, the fears, and the determination of people who had uprooted themselves completely in search of the promise of America. Most important, he was able to disclose the quiet dignity with which the majority of newcomers faced their considerable challenges.

Widely published in newspapers and magazines, the photographs changed many people's attitudes about the immigrants. But for Lewis Hine, an even greater photographic undertaking lay ahead.

Many of the immigrants Hine had photographed, along with hundreds of thousands of native-born Americans, had gone to work in the nation's ever-growing factories. Thousands of other Americans labored in such places as mines and canneries. These workers toiled long hours for very little pay. In order to survive, many families had to put their young children to work full-time.

It was a national disgrace. In 1901, when Hine began taking his immigrant pictures, some two million children, many younger than ten years old, were working from sunup to sundown in the nation's factories, mines, quarries, and canneries. Not only were they being denied schooling and the pleasures of childhood, but the tasks they carried out were physically dangerous. Child factory workers, forced to operate heavy machinery, often fell victim to serious accidents. Children working amid the coal dust of the mines suffered lung disease. Almost all the youngsters experienced the health problems associated with lack of sunlight and fresh air.

Among Hine's most telling child labor pictures were those taken of young children who spent ten hours a day, six days a week working in coal mines. All the youngsters in this photograph were under eleven years of age.

By the early 1900s, several reform groups had been formed to demand an end to child labor. The most important of these was the National Child Labor Committee (NCLC) which, in 1907, received a charter from Congress to pursue its goals. Some of the members of the committee had seen Hine's immigrant pictures. Impressed by the impact of the images, they asked him if he would be willing to leave his teaching position to document child-labor practices across the nation for them.

For Hine, it was an easy decision. He had become determined to carve out a career for himself as a full-time photographer, and equally important were his strong feelings about child labor. He had been orphaned at a young age and forced to support himself by working at a number of arduous, low-paying jobs. Fortunately he had been able to go to school when not at work. The plight of child laborers, who were even more deprived than he had been, struck home. Announcing to the committee that the motto of his photographs would be "Let the children be children," he accepted their offer.

For the next ten years Hine traveled across the country—in some years more than fifty thousand miles—photographing working conditions in all types of industries. He took pictures of child workers in textile mills, in meat-packing and cigar-making factories, in coal mines, and almost every other place where young children were employed.

Owners of the businesses that utilized child labor were determined to keep all reformers out of their establishments, particularly anyone armed with a camera. To gain entry into these places Hine often pretended he was either a Bible or an insurance salesman. Sometimes he got in by saying he was a photographer assigned to take pictures of factory machinery.

Hine spent as much time documenting his photographs as he did taking them. A skilled writer, he wrote detailed and moving notes on his young subjects, describing

After encountering one of Hine's pictures of children working in a textile factory, a South Carolina newspaperman wrote, "I'll never be able to put on a piece of clothing again without wondering if it was made with the sweat and tears of youngsters who should have been studying and playing in school."

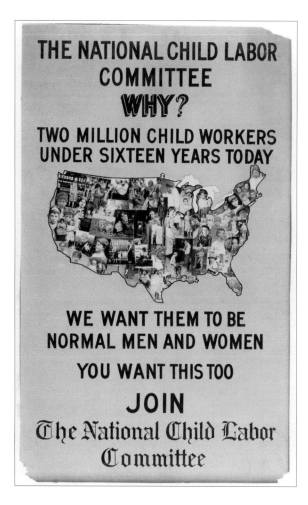

THE NATIONAL CHILD LABOR
COMMITTEE
WHY?
TWO MILLION CHILD WORKERS
UNDER SIXTEEN YEARS TODAY

WE WANT THEM TO BE
NORMAL MEN AND WOMEN
YOU WANT THIS TOO
JOIN
The National Child Labor
Committee

Among the most effective strategies used by the National Child Labor Committee to abolish child labor was the use of Lewis Hine's photographs in posters that were displayed throughout the country.

their age, the type of work they did, and the hardships and dangers they endured. These descriptions were almost as important as the photos themselves in convincing government officials and the American public that the evils of child labor were all too real.

Printed in newspapers and magazines throughout America, Hine's photographs were also used on posters, in booklets, and in films. Viewers, including government officials, were shocked by what his camera had revealed. They were also amazed at the quality of the images, particularly by the way Hine had been able to compose the photographs so effectively even while taking them under challenging conditions.

In 1916, thanks in great measure to Hine's photographs, Congress passed the first of several acts that set a minimum age for workers and a maximum number of hours a

Hine occasionally took pictures of youngsters in happier situations, such as this one of a New York City stickball game, to alleviate the sadness and outrage he felt in encountering children in unpleasant circumstances.

teen to work at night. In the years that followed, state legislatures, also influenced by Hine's pictures, passed even stricter laws banning child labor. By 1920 the number of child workers in the United States had been reduced to half of what it had been when Hine began his work. As Owen Lovejoy, the top official of the NCLC, stated, "The work that [Lewis Hine] did . . . was more responsible than any or all other efforts to bring the facts of child labor . . . to public attention."

By 1920 Lewis Hine's child-labor pictures had earned him fame as both a photographer and a reformer. A less dedicated person might easily have rested on his laurels and taken time to recover from the physical ordeal of having traveled so many miles and taken so many pictures under the most trying circumstances. But Hine felt that his work was not yet done.

Just as he was passionate about doing all he could to abolish the abuses of child labor, Hine was also fascinated by the way American workers were turning the United States into an industrial giant. He was determined to follow up his earlier success by taking photographs that celebrated work in general and the American worker in particular.

Beginning in the 1920s, and continuing well into the 1930s, Hine took thousands of photographs that he called work portraits. The most ambitious of these pictures were the spectacular images he captured of the creation of the Empire State Building. Designed to be the colossus of the New York City skyline, the Empire State Building was 102 stories high, the tallest building in the world at that time. Hine documented every foot of its construction. In order to capture his images of the workers as they toiled

The many photographs that Hine took of the construction of New York's towering Empire State Building represented his personal tribute to what he regarded as the backbone of American achievement—honest, legitimate labor.

on narrow girders or swung out on steel cables high above the ground, Hine was forced to take as many risks as the workers themselves. Camera in hand, he regularly swung out from the building in a specially designed basket one thousand feet above New York's Fifth Avenue.

The pictures he took proved to be more than just a glorification of what many regarded as a construction miracle. They spoke even more about the skill and integrity of the workers than the building itself. Just as Hine had been able to capture the tragic impact of child labor in the faces of the young workers he photographed, his pictures of the Empire State Building workers revealed the pride they took in what they were accomplishing.

When the construction project was complete, Hine published many of the photographs along with a few other work portraits he had taken in a picture book titled *Men at Work*. The pictures, taken at a time before working people became a fashionable subject of photographic studies, had a powerful impact upon the nation. As one newspaper proclaimed, "Lewis Hine has done nothing less than change the way Americans view the working class."

Late in his career, Lewis Hine was asked to describe what his goal had been. Without hesitation he replied, "I wanted to show the things that needed to be corrected; I wanted to show the things that needed to be appreciated." He did both. And by doing so, he brought about the changes he sought while inspiring generations of future photographers to follow in his path.

Haunting pictures of exploited children not only led to needed change, but also made Lewis Hine one of America's most respected photographers.

Edward S. Curtis

(1868–1952)

Immortalizing the Native Americans

But Edward S. Curtis accomplished it. That goal was, as he stated, "to form a comprehensive and permanent record of all the important tribes of the United States that still retain to a considerable degree their primitive customs and traditions."

Born near Whitewater, Wisconsin, in 1868, Curtis moved to Minnesota with his family when he was very young. His father had served with the Union army in the Civil War and had brought a camera back home

Edward Curtis began his career as one of thousands of commercial photographers in the United States.

with him when he returned. Although still a child, Curtis became fascinated with the device, built his own camera, and started taking pictures.

When he was nineteen, the family moved again, this time to a farm on Puget Sound in Washington State. A year later Curtis opened his own photography studio in nearby Seattle. Within a year, it became the busiest and most successful interested in them. He had photographed several Native Americans in his studio. Soon he began taking pictures of them as they dug for clams and mussels on the tidal flats of Puget Sound.

Curtis began to gain the trust of the wary tribal people of the area, particularly an aged woman nicknamed "Princess Angeline" by whites. She was the daughter of Sealth, the Suquamish chief after whom Seattle had been named. As he photographed her, Curtis saw in her face the suffering of a people displaced, but also a sense of pride and dignity.

This realization was the turning point in Curtis's life, for he came to understand that despite their determination to carry on their traditions, the ways of life of the Suquamish and all the other Native-American cultures throughout the nation were rapidly disappearing. He knew that if these ways of life were not recorded immediately, they would be lost to history for all time.

He was aware of something else as well. A great many Americans had negative feelings about Indian people because the books, newspapers, and magazines of the time often portrayed them as warlike, unfeeling people. Their deep-rooted traditions and spiritual feelings were practically unknown to the United States' non-Native population.

Curtis's portrait of Princess Angeline, taken early in his career, shows the young photographer's ability to show the very soul of his subjects.

Based on this knowledge, Curtis came up with an ambitious plan. He would leave his

Through pictures such as this one that he included in his twenty-volume publication titled The North American Indians, *Edward Curtis earned widespread acclaim.*

studio behind and try to reach as many Native Americans as he could. Once he encountered them, he would do his best to gain their trust and take as many pictures as possible of such things as their ceremonies, their dress, their dwellings, and, as Curtis put it, "their life and manners." He would also bring along sound equipment to record as many traditional tales and songs as he could. And, as if this was not challenging enough, he would culminate the project by putting together a large series of books containing thousands of his pictures and observations.

Curtis was not the first photographer to become obsessed with the idea of capturing the likenesses and the customs of the Native Americans for posterity. Others such as Adam Vroman, Roland Reed, and Ben Wittick also had this goal. But all these photographers had concentrated on one or two tribes. None had even thought of attempting to photograph as many tribes as they could reach. When Curtis informed officials at the Smithsonian Institution in Washington, D.C., of his plan, the experts there told him that his goal was impossible and that it would take fifty men more than five years to accomplish it.

But he was not to be deterred. Aided by a group of assistants, he set out on his daunting project. Before attempting to photograph a tribe, Curtis spent weeks reading all he could about the people's history and customs. Then he sent his assistants ahead of him to interview tribal members so that he knew even more about them when he reached their camp. Finally he traveled to a camp either on horseback or in a horse-drawn wagon and conducted interviews himself. All this before he took a single picture.

It was a painstaking procedure, but it brought great results. The care that Curtis took in making sure he understood the Native Americans he photographed did not go unnoticed by them. The people who had previously come to take their pictures had usually done so without any sense of their culture and with an eye toward quick profit. As Curtis said in his diary, "The ordinary investigator goes among them to secure information for a magazine article they do not favor. But they have grasped the idea that this is to be a permanent memorial of their race. Word passes from tribe to tribe about it. Tribes that I won't reach for four or five years yet have sent me word asking me to come and see them."

Curtis's diary also revealed how extraordinarily dedicated he and his staff were. "Breakfast hour was 7:30; beginning active work at 8:00, a half-hour for lunch, an hour for supper, then working until 1:00 A.M.," he wrote. "This was done every day of the month until spring. I permitted mail to come to our camp but once a week and no newspapers were allowed. Every thought and every movement had to be given to the work."

There were plenty of hardships, but Curtis never lost track of his goal. Cheyenne, Arapaho, Atsina, Yakima, Klickitat—he photographed people of all these tribes. Working with a huge fourteen-by-seventeen-inch camera, he captured thousands of dramatic scenes and portraits: chiefs on horseback, tribal members in front of tepees, ceremonial dances, hunting and fishing parties, haunting pictures of individual men, women, and children.

Perhaps the most telling of all the tens of thousands of Curtis's images is the one he called "The Vanishing Race." By photographing a column of Native Americans lost in the shadows, Curtis produced a picture symbolizing nothing less than his reason for his having undertaken his project. "The thought that this picture is meant to convey," he wrote, "is that the Indians as a race, already shorn of their tribal strength . . . are passing into the darkness of the unknown future."

Curtis's photograph of Hopi women climbing to their pueblo dwelling is a prime example of his determination to document "the old-time Indian, his dress, his ceremonies, his life and manners."

By taking several pictures of Native Americans moving away with their backs to his camera, Curtis gave dramatic voice to his sadness over what he saw as the Indians' vanishing ways of life.

Curtis felt that each of his photographs illustrated "some vital phase in [the subject's] existence."

Curtis had begun his career as a portrait photographer, and his other pictures also disclose his particular genius for this aspect of picture-taking. Time and again the portraits he made of the Indians, like those he had taken earlier of Princess Angeline, went beyond simple likenesses. As one photography critic has stated,

"Curtis worked as a [mapmaker], reading each face as a map of the past and of the character of each sitter. Unlike other Indian photographers . . . [he] sought always to bring out the individual qualities of the men, women, and children before his lens."

In 1930 an exhausted Edward Curtis finally completed his project. He had thought that it would take him five years to complete it. It took him more than thirty. He visited tribes ranging from the Eskimo and Inuit of Alaska and the Pacific Northwest to the Hopi of the Southwest. He photographed and recorded individuals of more than eighty different Indian groups. He had been able to continue his work through the financial help of wealthy financier J. P. Morgan. He had sacrificed his health, his own financial security, and his home life, but his achievement was monumental. He had photographed every major Native-American tribe west of the Mississippi, and had taken some forty thousand pictures. As if this were not amazing enough, he had also collected at least three hundred fifty traditional folk tales and stories and had made more than ten thousand recordings of Native-American languages and music.

But his work was not yet done. He still had to complete the last book in his multivolume set. It took him longer than a year to do so, but finally the series was finished. Titled *The North American Indian*, it was nothing short of mind-boggling: twenty huge, beautifully bound volumes containing Curtis's observations and pictures, each accompanied by a portfolio of large individual prints. In his foreword to the first volume of the set, former president Theodore Roosevelt praised Curtis for doing "what no other man has ever done; what, as far as we can see, no other man could do."

There was some negative criticism as well. Despite all the research he had conducted before

Many of the photographs Curtis took were created in what was known in his day as the pictorial approach: pictures that were as artistic in style as they were important in content.

taking his pictures, and all the care he had taken in portraying Native-American people, some critics were concerned that he had dressed his subjects in long-vanished trappings of earlier days. Curtis readily admitted doing so, explaining that by the time he had reached certain tribes their ways of life had been drastically altered by white culture, and he had wanted to portray the original Indian traditions.

Curtis achieved arguably the greatest single accomplishment in the annals of photography. But his legacy goes even deeper, for it was Edward Curtis who changed the nation's perceptions and attitudes about the very first Americans.

Edward Curtis captured some of the most beautiful images of Native Americans ever recorded.

James Van Der Zee

(1886–1983)

Revealing African-American Achievement

"You will not see the common images of black Americans,"

Van Der Zee's photographic studio was one of the most elegant in the country.

said the photography historian Reginald McGhee after he had viewed thousands of pictures taken by renowned African-American photographer James Van Der Zee. "You will not see downtrodden rural or urban citizens," McGhee promised. "Instead you will see a people of great pride and fascinating beauty."

Born in 1886, Van Der Zee grew up in Lenox, Massachusetts, which at that time was a summer retreat for wealthy New Englanders. His parents, who had been servants of Ulysses S. Grant when he was president, were better off financially than most African Americans of their day, and Van Der Zee was raised in a house filled with music and art.

When he was fourteen, Van Der Zee read a magazine advertisement that would change his life. The company that placed the ad stated it would send a box camera to anyone who sold twenty packets of its perfumed powder. The camera Van Der Zee received proved to be worthless, but the book of instructions that accompanied it fascinated him. He soon bought a better camera and began taking pictures of his friends and family.

At the age of twenty, Van Der Zee moved to a section of New York City called Harlem. There he founded a five-piece orchestra, but when that failed he earned his living as both a waiter and an elevator operator. In 1915 he moved to Newark, New Jersey, where he took a job as a darkroom assistant in a portrait studio.

The owner of the studio eventually noticed that Van Der Zee was skilled with a camera. Whenever he had to be away from his establishment, he put Van Der Zee in charge of taking the portraits. Soon customers began to notice that the pictures Van Der Zee took were far better than those taken by the owner.

In 1917, encouraged by this success, Van Der Zee, along with his second wife, Gaynella, opened his own establishment in Harlem, which he named the Guarantee Studio. He could not have chosen a more exciting place or time to launch his own photography career.

In the early decades of the twentieth century, Harlem was a remarkable and important place that would soon have a profound cultural influence throughout the United States and around the world. It was in Harlem that black writers, artists, poets, composers, singers, actors, and musicians gathered together to create what became known as "the cultural capital of black America." Included among these highly talented people were such writers as Langston Hughes and W. E. B. Dubois, actors such as Paul Robeson, artists such as Jacob Lawrence and William H. Johnson, dancers such as Josephine Baker, and singers and musicians such as Louis Armstrong, Fats Waller, and Billie Holiday.

Through pictures like this one of a successful professional dancer, Van Der Zee presented a much different portrayal of African-American life than most white people had seen.

The combination of these enormously creative talents led to such a flowering of African-American artistic expression and social thought that it became known as the Harlem Renaissance. The fact that life in Harlem provided most blacks who lived there with unprecedented independence and freedom of movement led to another important development as well. Thousands of African Americans, inspired by what was taking place in Harlem, began migrating to the industrial centers of the North, especially New York City.

Van Der Zee had opened his Harlem studio in order to earn what he hoped would be a good living. But he also recognized another opportunity. To him, photographing during such a historic time in African-American experience presented the chance to reveal through his pictures a different class of black people, more cultured and much more successful, than was commonly portrayed.

The studio itself reflected his goal of introducing the nation to a new type of black American. Unlike almost any other photography establishment that catered to blacks, it was elegantly adorned with expensive chairs, tables, drapes, floral arrangements, and richly illustrated backdrops.

Even more important was the care with which he took his pictures. Unlike most other portrait photographers of his day, Van Der Zee was intent on not merely producing a perfect likeness of his subjects but on capturing what it was that made each person who sat for him distinct. "I posed everybody according to their type and personality, and therefore almost every picture was different," he would later state. "In the majority of studios, they just seem to pose everybody according to custom, according to fashion, and therefore the pictures seem to be

Harlem was home to African Americans with diverse talents and beliefs, including members of a black Jewish congregation whom Van Der Zee photographed in front of their synagogue.

mechanical looking to me . . . I tried to pose each person in such a way as to tell a story."

Such dedication was grueling. Van Der Zee spent so much time posing and lighting each subject that he often could not produce more than three or four pictures that satisfied him in a day. But his commitment to his goal paid off. The men and women of Harlem—both unknown citizens and celebrities—flocked to his studio. Van Der Zee photographed them all, including society ladies in their beautiful clothes, wedding parties, and family groups. Among the scores of African-American

celebrities who sat before his camera were heavyweight-boxing champion Jack Johnson, famed dancer Bill "Bojangles" Robinson, and the Reverend Adam Clayton Powell.

Van Der Zee's celebrity portraits resulted in nothing less than a gallery of black achievement and pride. Equally important were the thousands of photographs he took outside his studio. The dedication he displayed in taking his portraits was now brought to the streets and buildings of Harlem. There he captured the life of the forty-five-block city district in all its various aspects. He took pictures of parades, men's and ladies' social clubs, schoolchildren, and business, sports, and civic activities.

Some of his photographs were of unique subjects, such as those he took of black Jews who lived and worshiped in Harlem. Van Der Zee was also fascinated by the elegant funeral ceremonies that were part of Harlem life and produced a series of photographs depicting the rituals that accompanied these events. The series, which revealed the special spiritual values that African Americans placed on funerals, was eventually published in a book titled *The Harlem Book of the Dead*.

Van Der Zee also captured many images of Marcus Garvey, the most influential African-American leader of the 1920s. Head of the Universal Negro Improvement Association, whose goals included that of promoting the spirit of black pride, Garvey chose Van Der Zee to chronicle the activities of his organization.

Among Van Der Zee's pictures were two that, in the view of many photography critics, epitomize his success in counteracting the false and harmful depictions of African Americans so prevalent in his time. In 1932 he took a photograph of a pair of Harlem's fashionable citizens and their new automobile, which

Van Der Zee was fascinated with the controversial African-American leader Marcus Garvey and took many pictures of him and his dedicated followers.

For most of his career Van Der Zee worked in relative obscurity, but after his 1969 Harlem on My Mind exhibition many of his photographs, particularly this one, began to be included in photography shows.

he titled "A Couple Wearing Raccoon Coats with a Cadillac." The luxurious shiny vehicle, the couple's expensive fur coats, and their proud, confident expressions create a portrait that is the personification of the energy and optimism of the Harlem Renaissance.

In this photograph of a Harlem couple on their wedding day, Van Der Zee inserted a ghostly image of a child to suggest the happy family life that he wished for the newlyweds.

Van Der Zee's photograph "Wedding Day" reveals his desire to convey the importance of family values in the Harlem community. It is an image that also reveals his commitment to depicting African Americans as cultured and refined people.

By the time World War II ended in 1945, James Van Der Zee had been taking pictures for more than forty-five years. His portrait business in particular had earned him a better living than he might have once imagined. But with the end of the war came the introduction of efficient, easy-to-use personal cameras. People had much less need for professional studio portraits, and Van Der Zee's fortunes declined dramatically. In order to support himself, he was forced to shoot passport photos and to search for other photography jobs. At the same time, the glory days of Harlem came to an end.

During the next two decades things got even worse for Van Der Zee. By 1967 his work had fallen into obscurity, he had lost his studio, and he and his wife were living in poverty. In that same year, however, a photo researcher at the Metropolitan Museum of Art stumbled upon tens of thousands of Van Der Zee's photographs that had been given to the museum. In 1969 the Metropolitan staged a major exhibition titled Harlem on My Mind, which featured many of the images the researcher had found. Almost overnight Van Der Zee began to receive national attention, and his fortunes were reversed once again.

This photograph of an African-American singing group rehearsing was typical of pictures Van Der Zee took to document the creativity and vitality that characterized Harlem during the 1920s and '30s.

Harlem on My Mind had another result as well. During its three-month run, it drew more viewers than almost any other exhibition in the museum's history. Most visitors were white, but for the first time African Americans came to the Metropolitan not as janitors or other menial laborers but as patrons.

Although Van Der Zee was now eighty-two years old, the attention and acclaim that Harlem on My Mind brought him rekindled his career. Just as, some sixty years before, famous African Americans had flocked to his studio, modern-day black celebrities now sought him out to have their pictures taken, including such highly respected people as Muhammad Ali, Bill Cosby, Cicely Tyson, Ossie Davis, and Ruby Dee.

At ninety-two, Van Der Zee found himself still in demand. "The body wears out," he told a reporter, "but the mind doesn't need to." In his final years he received many honors. He was awarded two honorary doctorate degrees and was named an Honorary Fellow for Life by the Metropolitan Museum of Art. He was also invited to the White House, where he was presented with the Living Legacy Award by President Jimmy Carter.

James Van Der Zee died in 1983 at the age of ninety-six. He had taken close to a hundred thousand photographs in a career that spanned more than eighty years, one of the longest in the history of photography. Yet it was what these pictures conveyed that was his great legacy. By producing images of a people and a culture in transition, he helped change whites' attitudes about African Americans and what they could achieve. As one photography critic has stated, "It's hard to see Harlem through any other eyes."

Van Der Zee would not snap his shutter until he was completely satisfied that the image, such as this classroom shot, captured exactly what he wanted it to say.

Dorothea Lange

(1895–1965)

Bringing Relief to Millions

"Their roots were all torn out,"

wrote Dorothea Lange. "The only background they had was a background of utter poverty . . . I had to get my camera to register those things about those people that were more important than how poor they were—their pride, their strength, their spirit." The people Lange was talking about were the hundreds of thousands of Americans who, in the 1930s, had lost

"Pick a theme and work it to exhaustion," Dorothea Lange once stated. "The subject must be something you truly love or truly hate."

almost everything they owned when their once-rich farmland turned to dust. The pictures she took made the nation aware of their plight and earned her the title "humanitarian with a camera."

Born in Hoboken, New Jersey, in 1895, Dorothea Lange began her photography career in 1919, when she opened a portrait studio in San Francisco. Most of her clients were very rich, and by the end of the 1920s, her business was prospering. But despite the wealth of those who sat before her portrait camera, millions of people were suffering through one of the most difficult times in our nation's history. The collapse of the stock market in 1929 had led to the closing of thousands of businesses, throwing much of the country out of work. People who had been successful suddenly found they had no jobs and no money. Many became homeless, forced to wander the streets in search of work.

Although Lange continued to take portraits in the comfort of her studio, she grew increasingly aware of the predicament of these people. She began spending more and more time roaming the streets, photographing them. Actually, she had become bored with taking portraits of the rich. From the moment she started taking her street pictures, she realized that she had found her true purpose in photography. She would use her camera to draw attention to the heartbreaking situations of those caught up in what was now known as the Great Depression.

Lange threw herself into her newfound work with a passion. "It was her intention," said one of her close friends, "to motivate change with every picture she took." Soon Lange's photos succeeded in capturing the attention of officials in the government, particularly a man named Roy Stryker. He was head of the Historical Section of the Farm Security Administration (FSA). His job was to direct a group of some of the finest photographers in the country as they captured images documenting the effect of the Depression on one enormous segment of the population in particular: the farmers.

By 1933 American cities were feeling the full effect of the collapse of the stock market. But in the southern plains states another type of disaster was taking place. For two full years that 97-million-acre section of the country had gone without rain. The

Lange was deeply touched by the victims of the Depression, whom she photographed in San Francisco before joining the FSA.

drought was so severe that the once-rich topsoil in such states as Oklahoma, Kansas, Texas, Colorado, and New Mexico turned to dust. When the dust was lifted into the air by the relentless prairie winds, huge storms were created that transformed the entire region into a gigantic dust bowl.

With the soil gone, millions of people lost the farms that had been in their families for generations. Hundreds of thousands took to the road and headed west to California and Oregon, looking for work picking fruit and vegetables. It was a terrible situation that got even worse when, after making the difficult journey, most of the migrants found little work for them to do—and what there was paid extremely low wages.

Clearly something had to be done. But before that could happen, the government had to be made fully aware of just how desperate the situation had become. That was why the FSA had been created. It was also why Roy Stryker, impressed with Lange's pictures of the disadvantaged people in San Francisco, offered her a job with his team. What Stryker could not know at the time was that Lange would produce many of the most important pictures of the entire photographic project.

Lange began her work with the FSA in 1935. For the next six years she photographed the Dust Bowl victims in twenty-two states. She captured images of families on the road in their battered cars as they tried to make their way west. She photographed them in the tent camps they set up once they reached the fields and orchards. And she took pictures of them as they picked the crops.

In the 1930s, as many as six thousand migrants made their way from the Dust Bowl to California every month; all became potential subjects for Lange's camera.

From the moment Lange began taking photographs of the dispossessed people of the Depression, she was aware of the importance of her pictures. She knew there were people who had criticized the FSA project, stating that it was really a propaganda campaign on behalf of the government's relief programs. Lange actually welcomed the criticism. By this time she had become convinced that the highest purpose to which the camera could be put was that of bringing about needed change. To Lange, propaganda, put to the right purpose, was both useful and necessary. "Everything," she later wrote, "is propaganda for what you believe in actually. I don't see that it could be otherwise. The harder and more deeply you believe in anything, the more in a sense you're a propagandist . . . I have never been able to come to the conclusion that [*propaganda* is] a bad word."

Lange was also aware that in order to get the type of images she desired, she would have to earn the trust of the Dust Bowl victims. "I had begun to talk to people I photographed," she later explained. "For some reason, I don't know why, the people in the city were silent people, and we never spoke to each other. But in the migrant camps, there were always talkers. This was very helpful to me, and I think it was helpful to them. It gave us a chance to meet on common ground."

Lange's friend Roy Partridge described how she put this approach into practice. "She would walk through the field and talk to people, asking simple questions. What are you picking? . . . How long have been here? When do you eat lunch? . . . 'I'd like to photograph you,' she'd say, and by now it would be 'Sure, why not,' and they would pose a little, but she would sort of ignore it, walk around until they forgot [her] and were back to work. Then she would begin to take her pictures."

The photographs she took in the fields and camps and on the roads captured not only the fear and despair experienced by her subjects, but also the dignity and courage with which most of them endured the conditions that had been

"I am trying here to say something . . . about the defeated, the alienated . . . about the last ditch," explained Lange.

forced upon them. Above all there was a compassion and sensitivity in the pictures that lifted them above simple documents of a particular time and place.

Much of this sensitivity was spawned by Lange's own difficult childhood. She'd had a bout with polio at the age of seven that had left her with a permanent limp, and her father had abandoned her mother and her when she was twelve; both events undoubtedly helped her understand the suffering of others. Her experience in meeting and photographing the homeless and jobless in San Francisco had also affected her profoundly. Whatever the cause, Lange's pictures reveal that she cared deeply about the people she depicted.

Nowhere is this more evident than in the picture Lange took of a mother and her three children seated in a tent in a migrant workers' camp. "I did not ask her name or her history," said Lange. "She told me her age, that she was thirty-two. She said that they had been living on frozen vegetables from the surrounding fields and birds that the children killed. She had just sold the tires from the car to buy food. There she sat in that lean-to tent with her children huddled around her, and seemed to know that my pictures might help her, and so she helped me. There was a sort of equality about it." The photograph, which Lange titled "Migrant Mother," is today regarded not only as the most outstanding of all the Depression-era pictures but also as one of the most powerful photographs ever taken.

Of all the people Lange photographed she was most taken with the women and the way in which, despite all that had been lost, they were determined to hold their families together. "Migrant Mother" was but one of hundreds of photographs Lange took of farm wives and mothers, women who she was convinced were the backbone of the nation. "These are women of the American soil," she said. "They are a hardy stock.

Lange's "Migrant Mother" photograph is perhaps the most famous image of the Great Depression.

They are the roots of our country. . . . They are not our well-advertised women of beauty and fashion. . . . These women represent a different mode of life. They are of themselves a very great American style. They live with courage and purpose, a part of our tradition."

Shortly after they were taken, "Migrant Mother" and scores of other Lange photographs were widely published in newspapers and magazines. The pictures quickly captured the attention and emotions of the entire country. One of the immediate results brought about by the pictures was that local and national government officials, shocked by the conditions under which the displaced families were living, immediately began erecting migrant camps to house them. These camps contained running water, toilet facilities, and other necessities that were sorely lacking in the places where the migrants were first forced to live. Most important, Lange's photographs called attention to a human disaster that, in the words of one congressman who saw them, "must never be repeated in this country again." Soon Congress began passing relief bills aimed at supplying financial aid to Dust Bowl victims.

The photographs triggered other results as well. The pictures that Lange had taken early on of the family farms turned to dust, for example, had a special impact. Government agricultural experts began initiating programs designed to teach southwestern farmers how to prevent the soil erosion that had brought on the disaster. Farmers learned how to rotate crops so that those that robbed the soil of nutrients would not be planted year after year. They were also taught which crops were actually beneficial to the soil.

Lange tirelessly photographed Depression victims throughout twenty-two states because she felt "one should really use the camera as though tomorrow you'd be stricken blind."

Lange had a special ability to tell a story with each photograph she took.

Lange's photographs also affected the world of literature. Author John Steinbeck was so moved by the images that he was motivated to write *The Grapes of Wrath*, regarded as one of the most powerful books ever published about the human condition.

And of course Lange's pictures had a profound effect on the world of photography. Dozens of young photographers, influenced by the power of her images and

This family made their way across the country by foot because they were too poor to own an automobile.

the changes they inspired, began taking pictures to depict examples of other conditions they felt needed correcting.

For Lange, the success of the Dust Bowl pictures was an affirmation of what she believed was photography's greatest gift: its ability to change the way people viewed the world. "The camera," she stated, "is an instrument that teaches people how to see without a camera."

Lange's ability to capture all moods of the Depression is what gives her work such lasting power.

Marion Post Wolcott

(1910–1990)

Introducing America to Americans

"I was committed to changing the attitudes of people,"

Marion Post Wolcott's assignments for the FSA took her from the dust of the drought-stricken areas to the deep snows of New England.

said Marion Post Wolcott, "by familiarizing America with the plight of the underprivileged, especially rural America." She did just that, and by doing so fulfilled one of the Farm Security Administration's missions. But the agency had another important goal as well, one inspired by its director, Roy Stryker.

Aware that he had assembled a team that included many of the country's most talented photographers, Stryker saw a rare opportunity. "One of our goals," he said, "will be to introduce America to Americans." By taking her camera to more places throughout the United States than any other FSA photographer, and by taking pictures not only of those caught up in hard times but of people in much different circumstances, Wolcott, more than any of her colleagues, produced a portrait of an America that few of its citizens had ever seen before.

Marion Post Wolcott was born in Montclair, New Jersey, in 1910. When she was a teenager her parents divorced, and her mother soon became the most influential person in her life. She was a highly cultured woman who introduced her daughter to the worlds of music, art, and the theater. She was also a social activist who worked for Margaret Sanger, one of the leaders of the early women's rights movement. It was from her mother that Wolcott inherited what was to become a lifelong passion for promoting positive social change.

In her early years Wolcott also had another personal relationship that would come to affect her thoughts and actions. Her mother had a black housekeeper with whom Wolcott developed a deep friendship, one that gave her a compassion for African Americans that would later influence many of the pictures she took.

When she finished high school, Wolcott went to New York University, where she studied to be a teacher. Upon graduation she took a job in a small private school in Massachusetts. But it was 1931, the nation was now fully enveloped in the greatest economic depression in its history, and, because of a lack of funds, the school was abruptly forced to shut down. Looking about for something to do, Wolcott discovered that her older sister Helen, who was pursuing a career in photography, was about to leave for Europe to study with the well-known Austrian photographer Trude Fleischmann. Wolcott joined her sister on the trip, a decision that would change her life.

While in Europe, Wolcott studied both dance and child psychology, but she also bought her first camera. She taught herself to use the device and was thrilled when Trude Fleischmann told her that she had "a good eye" and that she owed it to herself to continue photographing.

Her time in Austria, however, was also marked by much less pleasant experiences. The country had come under the control of the Nazis, and increasingly she and her sister witnessed brutal attacks on the nation's Jewish citizens. Appalled by what they saw and fearing for their own safety, Wolcott and her sister returned to America.

Back in the United States, Wolcott landed a teaching job at a prestigious private school in upstate New York. She also found herself spending more and more time taking pictures. After a year at the school she decided to take a bold step. She would

Wolcott's affinity for children led her to photograph youngsters throughout the nation, such as these pupils in a rural school in Kentucky.

Wolcott had a talent for capturing the emotions etched on the faces of her subjects.

give up teaching, move to New York City, and find out if she could succeed as a photographer.

She started out by freelancing and was delighted when she was able to sell several of her photographs to leading magazines. In 1935 she moved to Philadelphia, where she accepted a position as a staff photographer for the *Philadelphia Evening Bulletin*. She had hoped the job would give her the opportunity to capture images of the human condition, the type of pictures she was most interested in taking. Instead, as the newspaper's only female photographer, she found herself constantly assigned to do fashion photographs and other pictures for the "ladies' pages."

While freelancing in New York, Wolcott had attended meetings of the New York Photo League, where she became friendly with the noted photographer and filmmaker Ralph Steiner. Later, on a visit to New York while working at the *Bulletin*, Wolcott told Steiner how frustrated she was with her job at the newspaper. He, in turn, borrowed some of her photographs and took them to Washington, D.C., where he showed them to his friend Roy Stryker. Impressed with the pictures, Stryker immediately hired Wolcott as a member of the FSA photography team.

It did not take Wolcott long to demonstrate to Stryker that she would be one of the most energetic and talented of his photographers. It was clear that she had both the determination and the ability to incorporate the pictures she took of Depression victims with those that presented a wide-ranging portrait of American life.

Over the next three and a half years, Wolcott took picture after picture, many of which are among the most moving of the more than one hundred thousand images captured by the FSA photographers. Traveling backroads and highways, Wolcott shot in almost every part of the country. Nearly all the pictures she took reflected both her desire for constructive social change and her sensitivity to the feelings of those she photographed. The range of her pictures was truly astounding. Farmers, miners, steelworkers, white families at church suppers, black couples dancing at clubs called juke joints, children walking barefoot to school, fish fries, baptisms, southern barbecues, New England blizzards, Montana harvests—Wolcott photographed them all.

Among the photographs were many that were far different from those normally taken by the FSA photographers. Wolcott's subjects were not only the rural poor but the urban upper middle class and the wealthy. She realized that they, too, were an important part of introducing America to Americans. She had another reason for including them as well, later stating that she "wanted to show the extent of the gap between the wealthy and the poor."

Traveling to so many places was an enormously difficult task. The physical hardships alone—mud, heat, mosquitoes, rattlesnakes, to name but a few—would have broken the resolve of a less dedicated person. Particularly difficult were Wolcott's experiences photographing in New England during the harsh winter months. But both Wolcott and Stryker were determined that their portrait of America would include New England winter scenes.

"Shall I even try to tell you the difficulties I ran into with equipment when the temperature was so low?" Wolcott wrote to the FSA director. "Everything stuck and just refused to operate at least half the time. I finally rigged up something which should help—have put a ski pole basket on each tripod leg so that they act like snow shoes and it doesn't sink in so easily."

This photograph of an elegantly dressed man standing in front of a luxurious Florida hotel was typical of the many pictures Wolcott took to reveal what she regarded as the imbalance of wealth in America.

120

As trying as the physical challenges were, even more difficult were the loneliness and the hardships that came from traveling alone. From the beginning, Stryker was concerned about sending a woman alone to the rural Deep South. The only other woman he had sent to photograph in the region was Dorothea Lange, but she had traveled with her husband. Stryker's concerns were not unfounded.

As Wolcott moved throughout the South, she came face-to-face with the taboos and prejudices of the day, particularly regarding a woman traveling on her own while performing what was commonly regarded at the time as "man's work." In one town she was arrested. In most others she could not go into a coffee shop without suffering insults from the women and crude remarks from the men she encountered. And despite her compassion for them, many of the people she sought to photograph treated her with suspicion.

But she would not be deterred. Even though it was against her nature, she turned the other cheek to the insults and crude remarks. She won over many of her subjects by becoming involved with their lives—helping them to pick crops, reading to their children, showing them her mysterious photographic equipment. After she had taken and developed a few pictures in each place, her task usually got easier, for even the most suspicious could see that her pictures never compromised people's pride or dignity.

Among the thousands of photographs Wolcott took there was one that she unhesitatingly claimed as her favorite. It is a picture of a black man going into a movie theater in Belzoni, Mississippi, through the upstairs entrance that African Americans were forced to use. Photographically it is an extraordinary image,

This photograph of a Natchez, Tennessee, woman carrying a huge bundle on her head was taken in direct response to one of the FSA's main goals, that of producing images of an America few of its citizens had ever seen.

123

dramatically revealing Wolcott's mastery of composition and the use of light and shadow. But what the picture conveyed, particularly to people in regions outside the segregated South, was even more important. Here was racial injustice personified. Here was a situation that cried out for change. Explaining her feelings about the picture, Wolcott said simply, "I think it says the most about me, about what I was trying to do and trying to say."

Despite the hardships she encountered, Wolcott's FSA experience brought her satisfaction in her accomplishments and led to many personal discoveries as well. One of the most rewarding of these was the fact that she, a born-and-bred city girl, fell in love with the American countryside. One of her FSA colleagues recalled watching her as she picked up a handful of Virginia farm soil, brought it to her nose, and smiled in delight at its rich, natural scent.

Even though such subjects were not high on the list of suggested shots that Roy Stryker sent her, she captured images of the surrounding landscape in every area in which she photographed. Her pictures of fertile fields in Kentucky, North Carolina, and Virginia, seemingly endless plains in the Midwest, snowcapped mountains in Montana and Colorado, and barn and farmhouse vistas in New England formed a valuable addition to her American portrait.

In 1941 Wolcott met, fell in love with, and married a handsome young government agricultural official. The woman who had traveled so far alone finished the assignment she was working on and left the FSA. She spent the next thirty years raising a family, rarely taking a photograph. It was an ironic ending to the story of a woman who had been totally consumed with taking pictures.

Like Dorothea Lange's "Migrant Mother" picture, Wolcott's masterful photograph of an African-American man approaching the "colored" entrance to a movie house became a symbol of the era in which it was taken.

Roy Stryker ordered the FSA photographers to "show the city people what it's like to live on a farm," a mandate that Wolcott carried out through pictures such as this one.

Yet what she accomplished in less than four years was remarkable. "We hoped we would change people's ideas and opinions by showing what the country was like," she stated in a 1988 television interview. "Fortunately we did it, because people will look at photographs when they won't read things. We had an impact."

By documenting the diverse ways of life of the nation's citizens, such as those involved in this Kentucky baptism, Marion Post Wolcott introduced Americans to their country.

Margaret Bourke-White

(1904–1971)

Celebrating Industrious America

"The camera is a remarkable instrument,"

said Margaret Bourke-White. "Saturate yourself with your subject, and the camera will all but take you by the hand and lead the way." During her career Bourke-White "saturated" herself with many subjects, and in the process of taking perhaps more pictures than any other news photographer in history she changed photography itself and the perceptions of many who saw her pictures.

She was born in New York City in 1904 and spent her child-

Operating in what was typically a man's world, Margaret Bourke-White became arguably the world's most prolific and well-known photographer.

hood in Bound Brook, New Jersey. After graduating from high school, she took a course in photography taught by master photographer Clarence White. Then she went off to college, still uncertain about what she wanted to do with her life.

It was while she was taking pictures for the school yearbook at the University of Michigan that she finally discovered her calling. Along with photographing her fellow students, she began capturing images of the many interesting buildings on campus, shooting them from as many interesting angles as she could. Bourke-

White found that she was not only excited by what her camera could produce, but by the way it could reveal what was, to her, the beauty to be found in man-made objects. "We all find something that is just right for us," she later wrote, "and after I found the camera I never really felt a whole person unless I was planning pictures or taking them."

In 1925 she transferred to Cornell University. While there, she spent most of her time taking pictures, and her work attracted the attention of several magazine editors. Before she graduated, Bourke-White experienced the thrill of having several of her pictures published. At the time, a major development was taking place in American art. Many painters and photographers who had previously focused on depicting scenes from nature were turning their attention to objects that to them personified what was becoming known as the Machine Age. Some had begun using their brushes and their cameras to portray the latest enormous structures and mechanical objects that were becoming the symbols of the United States as an industrial giant.

To Bourke-White, this new photographic approach, which would come to be known as industrial photography, spoke directly to the types of pictures she had begun taking while in college. To her, machines and structures—turbines, manufacturing plants, bridges, and dams—not only represented what had been achieved, but also suggested even greater advancements that lay ahead. And in her eyes, the shapes, forms, and textures of industrial objects, large and small, were as intriguing as almost any other subjects that had ever been photographed.

In 1927 Bourke-White graduated from Cornell and almost immediately received a photographic assignment that

Life magazine's first cover featured Bourke-White's image of Montana's Fort Peck Dam, a photograph that illustrated her belief that beauty could be found in man-made structures.

LIFE

NOVEMBER 23, 1936 **10** CENTS

would validate all her feelings about picture-taking. She was commissioned to take a series of photos of the vast steel mills in Cleveland, Ohio.

Bourke-White took dozens of photographs of the mills. She photographed their towering smoke-belching chimneys, the sprawling multishaped buildings, the lifelike cranes and derricks, and the long, narrow walkways that connected the structures. Inside the buildings, she took close-up pictures of the huge glowing furnaces and the many varied objects involved in the steel-making process.

She not only succeeded in producing the vital documentation that the owners of the steel mill had hired her to compile, but captured images that gave expression to her delight in taking the pictures. She knew she was onto something new and important, and she was able to state her feelings eloquently. "Any important art coming out of the industrial age," she wrote, "will draw inspiration from industry, because industry is alive and vital. The beauty of industry lies in its truth and simplicity. Every line is essential and therefore beautiful."

When the Cleveland pictures were published by the steel company, they attracted quite a lot of attention. Among the influential people most impressed with Bourke-White's photographs was Henry Luce, a publisher who had just launched a major new magazine. Called *Fortune* and destined to become the leading advocate of the machine age, the magazine was devoted to promoting the romance of industry. Luce hired Bourke-White and brought her to New York, where she became the publication's leading photographer.

Bourke-White's purpose in taking this dramatic photograph of massive ammonia gas tanks was to show that even the most enormous industrial objects could be controlled by humans.

Bourke-White took thousands of photographs for *Fortune* over the next several years. She took pictures of the meatpacking plants in Chicago, the stone quarries in Indiana, and the glassblowing factories in upstate New York, among scores of other subjects. She also captured compelling images of monumental bridges and majestic dams under construction.

In 1930 the magazine presented Bourke-White with the most challenging assignment she had ever received. She was sent to Germany to photograph the emerging industry there. She knew that what *Fortune* really wanted was pictures of Russia (officially the Soviet Union at this time), a nation that was in the midst of an industrial and cultural revolution. But she also knew that Russia's doors were closed to all foreigners, particularly photographers, and that the magazine was convinced no outsider toting a camera would be allowed to enter the country.

Bourke-White went to Germany and took her photographs. But while she was there, she began contacting Russian officials on her own, asking them to allow her to photograph the industrial progress being made. Her persistence paid off, and even though it took six weeks of pleading and convincing, she was finally able to get permission to go to Russia and take pictures. There were, however, still obstacles to overcome.

After packing up her camera equipment and stocking trunks with food, she entered Russia and headed for the new industrial areas by traveling on the long, still-primitive Trans-Siberian Railway. When she finally reached the first place where she wanted to take pictures, she ran into all kinds of resistance from local authorities. As she would do throughout her career, Bourke-White found a way to overcome this setback. She arranged for a meeting with a high-ranking Soviet offi-cial and showed him a number of her industrial photographs. The pictures so impressed him that he wrote out a special permit requiring Soviet citizens to help the American photographer in any way they could.

Bourke-White captured unique images in out-of-the-way places. Here, workers toil inside a caisson at Russia's Dneprostroi Dam.

In this photograph, Bourke-White paid homage to a great icon of the industrial age: New York's spectacular George Washington Bridge.

For the next five weeks Bourke-White traveled throughout Russia, taking photographs of factories, dams, farms, and Soviet workers. She took three thousand pictures in all, photographs that provided Americans and people from other nations with their first views of the newly emerging Russia.

Bourke-White continued to photograph for *Fortune* for three more years. By this time, many other photographers had started capturing images of the objects and structures of the industrial age. Some, most notably the artist/photographer Charles Sheeler, produced outstanding pictures in this genre. But Bourke-White's photographs stood out from all the rest. Perhaps it was because, as one photography critic has put it, "Almost every one of her images had a human, emotional quality about it even when no humans appeared in the picture."

Bourke-White's role in making Americans feel less threatened by and more appreciative of the huge changes being brought about by the industrial age was a major contribution to the country. But in producing her pictures for *Fortune*, she pioneered another important change as well. Many of her shots of a particular subject, such as the building of a dam or operations in a particular factory, were printed not alone but as a series of images. Presented sequentially, the pictures told a powerful story by themselves. They were so powerful, in fact, that increasingly *Fortune* used fewer and fewer words to accompany them. Eventually this type of presentation came to be called the photo-essay, and, in an age before television and computers, it revolutionized the way people received information.

The photo-essay was beginning to capture the attention of the public just as Henry Luce was founding a magazine even more far-reaching than *Fortune*. Called *Life*, its goal was to chronicle events from around the world through photo-essays, individual pictures, and words. Luce hired Bourke-White to take pictures for the new publication and, just as had taken place with the earlier magazine, she became *Life*'s leading photographer.

Life was launched in 1936, and for the next twenty years Bourke-White traveled the world taking photographs for what rapidly became the most widely read picture magazine in history. Her assignments took her to South Africa, where she compiled a photo-essay on black miners searching for diamonds deep within the earth, and to India, where she photographed Mohandas K. Gandhi just hours before the great leader was assassinated. The pictures she took in

Her belief that "utter truth is essential" led Bourke-White to capture images that were infused with a sense of humanity, such as this picture of miners in South Africa.

Czechoslovakia and Romania introduced *Life*'s readers to people and places previously unknown to them. She photographed almost every world leader and documented the lives of ordinary people around the globe.

When World War II broke out, Bourke-White became an official air force photographer through a special arrangement made with the Army Air Forces and took dramatic pictures of military campaigns in North Africa, Italy, and Germany.

Bourke-White's appreciation for the ironic led her to take pictures such as this one showing poor people in a bread line before a billboard praising America's quality of life.

Margaret Bourke-White traveled the world capturing unforgettable images, such as this sensitive portrayal of India's pacifist leader Mohandas K. Gandhi.

Bourke-White was the first woman authorized to fly on a combat mission, and was the only photographer from the West to capture images of Germany's aerial bombing of Moscow in 1941. At the close of the war she documented the horrors of the Nazi concentration camp at Buchenwald.

As a press journalist, Bourke-White took more pictures than any other photographer in history—more than two hundred fifty thousand photographs in all. Just as her early pictures were marked by the way she was able to reveal the beauty in industrial objects, her press photographs were characterized by her obvious concern for the human condition.

Technically, Margaret Bourke-White was a brilliant photographer. But the contributions she made to America came as much from the heart as from her hand and eye. Added to this was her fierce sense of purpose. "We as photographers," she wrote, "see a great deal of the world. Our obligation is to pass it on to others."

Millions of people around the world were unaware of the horrific Nazi concentration camps until they saw this photograph of the camp at Buchenwald.

Toni Frissell

(1907–1988)

Changing Attitudes About African Americans

"The story of my life is told in the photographs I have taken,"

"Each person has a contribution to make in life," said Toni Frissell's daughter Sidney. "[My mother's] contribution was her photography."

said Toni Frissell. "The places I have visited, and people I have met . . . the photographer's subjects help shape her destiny." Many photographers spend their whole careers concentrating on a single approach to the medium. Some master the art of portraiture. Others focus on photojournalism or documentary or war photography. Toni Frissell mastered all these fields.

Frissell was born in 1907 into a family of adventurers. Her grandparents had been pioneers, crossing the continent to settle in Oregon. One of her uncles had made the long trek to Alaska in search of gold. He had also sailed the seas in clipper ships and whaling vessels. Her older brother Varick would travel the world as an explorer, a mountain climber, and a filmmaker.

Despite this background, Frissell's early days gave little indication of the adventurous life she herself would come to lead. Her father was an extremely wealthy doctor, and Frissell's childhood and teenage years were filled with luxury. She spent her summers in Newport, Rhode Island, then one of the most popular playgrounds of the rich. Her days were spent playing tennis and swimming at exclusive clubs, and her evenings were filled with parties and balls at Newport's fabled mansions.

Frissell's life in the winter was not much different. The parties and balls continued. There was theater and opera to be enjoyed. And there was shopping. Even as a child, she loved to shop for clothes and look through fashion magazines. Although she could not know it at the time, it was a passion that would play an important role in her future.

As enjoyable as Frissell's early years had been, by the time she entered her twenties she began to be bored with her life of leisure. Searching for something more interesting to do, she tried her hand at acting. When her theatrical career proved far from spectacular, she decided to give it up. But almost immediately fate lent a hand in the form of her brother Varick, whom Frissell idolized. Standing six feet eight inches tall, he was a handsome young man, the leader of his large circle of friends. He had a rich singing voice and for a time considered pursuing a career in opera. But his ambitions changed when he went on an expedition to the Arctic. Fascinated with the area, he decided to do a documentary film on the seal fisheries there. He took many photographs for the film, and when he returned home he taught Toni how to take pictures.

The lessons would change her life, but not immediately, for soon tragedy struck. Not long after he introduced his sister to photography, Varick set sail again for the Arctic, intent on finishing his seal-fisheries film. Off Newfoundland, his ship was suddenly rocked by a series of explosions, and Varick was killed. It was a loss that Toni would feel for the rest of her days.

It was 1931 and Frissell was twenty-four years old. Realizing that the best way

By taking her models outside the studio, Toni Frissell changed the world of fashion photography.

to ease her sorrow was to do something productive, she sought out one of her friends who was an executive at *Vogue*, one of the nation's leading fashion magazines. Her friend hired her to write captions for pictures, but Frissell was not good at writing and soon lost her job. On the day she was fired, her friend gave her some important advice. "Toni," she said, "take up photography seriously. Your brother had such talent. Let me see what you can do."

That summer Frissell returned to Newport but this time not to play. She devoted almost all her energy to honing her photographic skills. When the summer ended she went back to *Vogue* and showed her friend the pictures she had taken. Highly impressed with the images, her friend rehired her, this time as a photographer.

Frissell went on to take photographs for *Vogue* for the next eleven years. During that time she also had special assignments for such leading magazines as *Harper's Bazaar*, *Vanity Fair*, and *Town & Country*. Her pictures not only revealed her unique photographic style, but also changed the entire world of fashion photography forever.

Before Frissell began her work for *Vogue*, almost all fashion photographs were taken indoors under heavy artificial lighting. Props and painted backdrops were sometimes used to simulate outdoor scenes, but neither the photographer nor the models left the studio. The resulting pictures were stiff and formal.

Toni Frissell changed all that. Intent on producing the most fascinating images she could create, she was the first to take her models outside to exotic places even when they were dressed in evening gowns or furs. "Instead of using studio lights," she would later write, "I took models to Peru, to Jamaica, to Guatemala, and the West Indies—always seeking out natural settings. I wanted them to look like human beings, with the wind blowing their hair and clothes. As a photographer I was most successful when I did things naturally."

Her success was also due to the fact that she was the first to realize that an outstanding fashion photograph is as much a picture of a woman as it is of a particular dress, gown, or coat. Her pictures were marked not only by their fascinating surroundings but also by the way she captured her models' personalities.

This striking shot of local fishermen was taken while Frissell was on a fashion shoot in the West Indies.

After more than a decade of taking her camera and her models around the world, the restless Frissell began to look for new realms to explore. "I became so frustrated with fashions," she stated, "that I wanted to prove to myself that I could do a real reporting job." While she was considering what to do next, events once again made her decision for her.

On December 7, 1941, the United States entered World War II. Frissell quickly contacted a U.S. Army official and offered her services to take pictures for the military. Thanks to the reputation she had built as a magazine photographer, she was immediately hired. She spent the entire five years of the conflict in Europe, capturing images of soldiers, airmen, civilians, and all those caught up in the war. Demonstrating the same energy she had displayed in changing the nature of fashion photography, she took pictures not only for the army, but also for the air force, the Women's Army Corps, and the Red Cross.

Like many of the other World War II photographers, she often found herself in real danger. Once, while photographing close to the battle lines in Germany, the jeep she and her driver were riding in was struck by shell fragments. The driver was wounded, but Frissell escaped; she was shaken but unharmed. On another occasion she talked her way into being allowed to accompany an infantry division as it attacked enemy forces. Her camera was always with her, and by the time the war finally ended in 1945 she had taken thousands of pictures.

Many of the images that Frissell captured are regarded as among the most powerful or most poignant of the war. Scores of them were published in such magazines as *Life*, *Collier's*, and *The Saturday Evening Post*. One picture in particular, that of a young boy sitting in the ruins of

Frissell's pictures of the mechanics attached to the Tuskegee squadrons showed that African Americans could maintain sophisticated fighter planes as well as fly them.

his bombed-out house, had a special impact. Describing the circumstances of the photograph, taken immediately after German bombs had destroyed an entire London neighborhood, Frissell stated, "A small boy was sitting at the bottom of a high pile of haphazard planks and beams. I was told he had come home from playing and found his house in shambles—his mother, father, and brother dead under the rubble. . . . He was looking up at the sky, his face an expression of both confusion and defiance. . . . His was the face of war."

While this picture turned out to be Frissell's most remembered war image, a special series of pictures she took was arguably the most important. When the conflict began, racial discrimination, which was widespread in America at the time, had prevented African Americans from being assigned meaningful roles in the armed forces. Many prejudiced people mistakenly felt that blacks would not be able to serve as ably as their white counterparts. Outraged civil-rights organizations had demanded that steps be taken to correct the situation. One of the most immediate results of the protests was the formation in 1941 of all–African American fighter squadrons. Because the squadrons were trained in Tuskegee, Alabama, the units, which included pilots, navigators, bombardiers, and mechanics, became known as the Tuskegee Airmen.

Despite the odds against them, the Tuskegee Airmen became one of the most highly respected fighter groups of World War II. Based in both North Africa and Italy, Tuskegee pilots and their crews flew more than seven hundred missions. They earned some 745 Air Medals, more than one hundred Flying Crosses, fourteen Bronze Stars, eight Purple Hearts, a Silver Star, and a Legion of Merit.

Frissell's unforgettable photograph of a child sitting outside the wreckage of his bombed-out house illustrates her belief that "The worst part of war is what happens to the survivors."

Toni Frissell's picture of two Tuskegee Airmen looking skyward can be seen as a symbol for the way that, through her photographs, she expanded the horizons of African Americans everywhere.

Toni Frissell was the first photographer permitted to take pictures of the Tuskegee Airmen in combat situations. She even flew aboard one of their fighter planes as it went out in search of enemy aircraft. Her pictures were widely published in newspapers, magazines, and military publications and went beyond documenting the

Frissell's ability to gain access to unique and important situations, such as her flights with the Tuskegee Airmen, was remarkable given that she was working at a time when most war photographers were men.

Airmen's accomplishments. By providing the visible evidence of the dedication, skill, and courage of the Tuskegee Airmen, she helped pave the way for blacks to enter all branches of the military and helped change many individuals' attitudes about what African Americans could accomplish if given the chance.

When World War II ended, Frissell was in great demand. Barely pausing to catch her breath, she began taking pictures and creating photo-essays for various national magazines. Among these publications was *Sports Illustrated,* which, by hiring Frissell, made her the nation's first female sports photographer. It was a new experience for Frissell, and one she loved.

Frissell was also highly skilled at taking compelling portraits. Her most memorable is one that she took of the great English wartime leader Sir Winston Churchill. Often a cantankerous man, Churchill hated sitting still for the camera. He had scared away almost every photographer who had tried to capture an official likeness of him. But when Churchill saw the picture that Frissell had taken, he was so impressed with it that he made it his official portrait.

By moving so far beyond the life of luxury into which she was born, Toni Frissell became one of the most innovative and versatile photographers of her time. In the process, she revolutionized a large field of photography and changed attitudes about the abilities of a huge segment of the American population.

Frissell was justifiably gratified by the result of her long and difficult picture-taking session with the often cantankerous British leader Winston Churchill.

NASA and NOAA

(Established 1958 and 1970)

Changing Our View of the Universe

"We are . . . humbled,"

said an official of NASA (the National Aeronautics and Space Administration), "by the realization that Earth is just a tiny 'blue marble' in the cosmos." He was summing up the discoveries made in the last four decades by its astronauts and scientists. Many of these discoveries have been made through the use of photography, which has given us the means to

America's astronauts have been acclaimed for their courage, but relatively little attention has been paid to the contributions they have made as photographers of unprecedented images such as this one of Earth as seen from space.

view not only ourselves and our world but also the universe in a whole new way.

In 1957 the Soviet Union shocked people everywhere by launching the world's first space satellite, Sputnik. The event caused particular alarm in the United States. American military leaders feared that the Soviet Union's now-proven ability to place objects in space would give that country a distinct military advantage over all others. American scientists were also concerned about losing scientific superiority to the Soviets.

As a direct result of Sputnik's launch, NASA was established, and the agency immediately began working to put not only satellites but also Americans in space. In addition, NASA officials stated that its other important goal was to lead the world in the "expansion of human knowledge of atmosphere and space."

It was an enormous undertaking. NASA's first task was to create and build the massive, sophisticated equipment needed to meet these goals. The agency selected the first group of astronauts who would lead America into space. The astronauts were then put through the most rigorous training program any individuals had ever experienced. Included in this training were hands-on practice in enduring the launch into space, controlling a space capsule in flight, living in a weightless state, and returning to Earth safely. Hours were also spent teaching the astronauts how to operate the lightweight, sophisticated cameras with which they would hopefully be able to record their accomplishments and even take pictures of Earth and other parts of the universe as seen from space.

NASA's first high-profile program was called Project Mercury. Its goals were to "place a piloted spacecraft into space, observe human performance in space, and recover the human and the spacecraft safely." On May 5, 1961, astronaut Alan Shepard became the first American to fly into space, but his flight did not take him around Earth. That feat was accomplished on February 20, 1962, when astronaut John Glenn successfully orbited Earth three times.

Project Mercury was followed by Project Gemini, which built upon Mercury's successes but used spacecraft carrying two astronauts rather than one. A major highlight of this program was the achievement of the first American space walk. The "walk" was taken by Gemini astronaut

On June 3, 1965, astronaut Edward H. White II, with his camera attached to the equipment in front of him, became the first American to step into space.

Edward H. White II, who stepped out of his space module on June 3, 1965. Along with his other equipment, White was armed with a camera, and during his twenty-three-minute, sixty-five-hundred-mile orbital stroll he took the first photographs ever produced by a photographer floating in space. They would be the first of thousands of pictures that astronauts who followed White would take from both inside and outside their spacecraft, photographs that would reveal whole new worlds.

Both Project Mercury and Project Gemini paved the way for Apollo. In May 1961, a year before John Glenn's historic achievement, President John F. Kennedy had thrilled Americans by announcing an astounding objective. "I believe," Kennedy said, "this nation should commit itself to achieving the goal, before this decade is out, of landing a man on the Moon and returning him safely to Earth. No single space project in this period will be more impressive to mankind, or more important in the long-range exploration of space."

To many, Kennedy's goal seemed impossible. Putting men into space was remarkable enough, but landing a man on the moon and bringing him back safely seemed almost unimaginable. Yet NASA accomplished it. On July 20, 1969, much of the world watched their television sets in amazement as Apollo 11 astronaut Neil Armstrong stepped onto the moon. "That's one small step for man; one giant leap for mankind," he proclaimed.

That same day, Armstrong and his fellow astronaut, Edwin "Buzz" Aldrin, began exploring the once inaccessible moon and collecting specimens from its surface. They also began taking photographs. These pictures and the thousands of others taken by astronauts on succeeding Apollo flights provided the world with

Photographs such as this one taken by James B. Irwin of his fellow astronaut David R. Scott provided new information about the moon.

new and vital information about the moon and its relation to Earth and the rest of the universe.

Buoyed by its Apollo success, NASA officials began looking beyond the moon to even more distant celestial bodies. Actually, exploration of such planets as Mercury, Venus, and Mars had begun as early as 1962 through the use of satellites outfitted with cameras. The first of these projects was named Mariner, and, between 1962 and 1973, NASA built and sent ten Mariner spacecraft to explore the inner solar system. These unmanned, camera-equipped craft flew past and around Mercury, Venus, and Mars, taking photographs that revealed many of these planets' craters, volcanoes, and valleys. Mariner cameras even captured images of cosmic rays produced outside the solar system. In the decades that followed the Mariner discoveries, NASA projects collected even more information about Mars, particularly once the agency succeeded in landing roving camera-equipped vehicles on the planet. Then, in 1996, NASA launched its Mars Global Surveyor (MGS), a spacecraft designed to take pictures and create maps of Mars for years to come.

Since the Mars Global Surveyor has been in operation it has produced a wealth of amazing images and has made a host of major discoveries. MGS photographs have given astronauts and scientists their first detailed understanding of the relative heights of various Martian geological features and have revealed what may well be the largest impact basin in the solar system. Most important, the continuous stream of pictures taken of Mars has shown that the planet is constantly reshaped by natural forces, including shifting sand dunes, enormous wind and dust storms, and polar ice caps that grow and recede with changing seasons.

Using extraordinary pointing precision, powerful cameras, and other optical equipment, the Hubble Space Telescope has provided stunning images of the universe.

In 2001, NASA launched the Mars Odyssey orbiter which, for several months, captured even more detailed images of the planet. Three years later, the greatest breakthrough of all took place. In 2004, NASA sent the Mars Spirit Rover and the Mars Spirit Opportunity to the so-called red planet. The unmatched imagery relayed to Earth from these two camera-equipped space detectives enabled scientists to study Mars as never before. The rovers' cameras provided many important pieces of information, including indisputable proof that large amounts of water once existed on Mars, raising the possibility that life was once possible on the distant planet.

Because of its many and varied large projects, NASA operates a host of space centers located throughout the nation. One of these, the Space Telescope Science Institute, is responsible for conducting and coordinating the operation of the Hubble Space Telescope. An astronomical marvel, the Hubble was first launched in 1990 and, as one agency official has stated, "Not since Galileo turned his telescope towards the heavens in 1610 has any event so changed our understanding of the universe."

Equipped with highly advanced cameras, Hubble orbits 375 miles above Earth, unlocking the secrets of the heavens. Circling Earth every ninety-seven minutes, Hubble has observed more than twenty-five thousand astronomical targets and has taken more than three hundred thirty thousand pictures. Before Hubble, distances to far-off galaxies were not well known. Answers to the vital question of just how rapidly the universe is expanding were even more elusive. The stunning images and other data provided by Hubble have changed all that.

The photographs taken by American astronauts have enabled them to visually document each space adventure, allowing them to evaluate the effectiveness of every vital piece of equipment used.

Hubble's cameras have given us the first clear images of Saturn's aurora in pictures that were taken when the planet was more than 800 million miles from Earth. Hubble's cameras have also allowed astronomers to peek into the center of a cluster of stars so densely packed that the stars occasionally collided. Called Omega Centauri, the cluster is located about seventeen thousand light-years from Earth. Cameras aboard the Hubble have also taken the first pictures of a gamma-ray burst, one of the most powerful explosions in the universe. And the near-infrared camera aboard the Hubble has penetrated layers of dust in a star-forming cloud to reveal, for the first time, the inner region of those enormous clouds of gas and dust in space known as nebulae.

The photographs captured by cameras operated either by NASA or by its many related agencies have not only changed our perceptions of the universe, but have also changed the way we view our own planet. Two projects in particular, Landsat (Land Remote Sensing Satellite) and GOES (Geostationary Operational Environmental Satellites) have made this possible. Landsat's remote-controlled satellites house cameras that continually provide data that is then converted into color photographs. Among their many uses, the pictures, taken far above Earth, help government and private organizations assess flood damage and plan disaster-relief and flood-control programs. Landsat images have also proven invaluable to mariners. By studying Landsat photographs, for example, ship owners and captains can avoid ice-covered ocean areas and can discover which ports are free of ice.

NASA's GOES program, administered by the National Oceanographic and Atmospheric Administration (NOAA), uses camera-equipped satellites to continuously

Among the most spectacular and important images captured by the cameras aboard the Hubble Telescope is this picture of Saturn, which reveals never-before-seen details of the planet.

monitor weather conditions in the western hemisphere, particularly unpredictable severe storms. Commonly featured on TV weather reports across the United States and the rest of the world, pictures provided by GOES accurately predict such natural phenomena as tornadoes, hurricanes, and flash floods. They have also become essential in monitoring dust storms, volcanic eruptions, and the spread of forest fires.

The photographs taken by our astronauts, the various camera-equipped satellites, and the Hubble Space Telescope have immeasurably advanced our knowledge of space. But there is another vast frontier that exists as well. It is the world that lies beneath the oceans, lakes, and seashores, a "final frontier" that, in the opinion of many scientists, has the potential to yield even more secrets and ultimately be of greater value than what has been discovered in space.

Just as NASA is responsible for our activities in space, NOAA is responsible for the "establishment of programs for the assessment, protection, development, and utilization of United States underwater resources." In order to fulfill this responsibility, NOAA established its NOAA Undersea Research Program (NURP), which operates out of six regional centers.

These centers conduct their research by placing American scientists under the sea in a variety of ways, including the use of scuba-diving equipment, manned underwater vehicles called submersibles, remotely operated underwater vehicles, and underwater laboratories. Along with conducting research that has already vastly expanded our scientific knowledge of the world beneath the sea, the centers continue to develop new technology designed to make underwater exploration increasingly productive.

Understanding that the world beneath the sea may eventually yield great benefits to humankind, scientists armed with cameras take pictures that will help them unlock the secrets of the deep.

Like the astronauts, many of the scientists who have probed the ocean, lake, and coastline floors

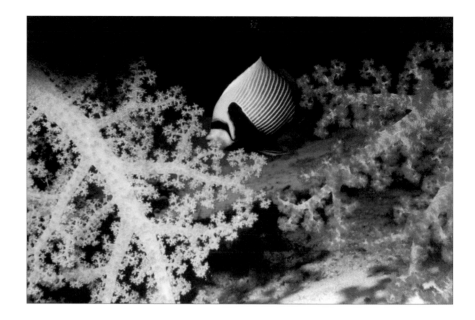

have been equipped with cameras. The photographs they have taken have provided vital new information about coral reefs, deep-water mountains and canyons, and undersea volcanoes. Their cameras have recorded the discovery of whole new ecosystems and previously unknown forms of fish and plant life.

Miles above the earth and miles below the seas, men and women equipped with cameras follow in the footsteps of incredible photographers who have come before—the people whose tireless work has changed the way we view our world and ourselves.

The photographs taken on the ocean's floor by scientists, like these two photos of coral reefs, are the latest in a long history of pictures that expand our knowledge of the world around us.

FURTHER READING

The books listed here provide further information about the photographers profiled in this book and about the story of photography and its importance to the world in general. Although some were written years ago, they are available in most public libraries. Readers can also find a wealth of information about each of the photographers by researching them through the Internet.

Alland, Alexander. *Jacob A. Riis, Photographer and Citizen*. Millerton, NY: Aperture, 1974.

Callahan, Sean, ed. *The Photographs of Margaret Bourke-White*. New York: New York Graphic Society, 1980.

Coles, Robert. *Dorothea Lange: Photographs of a Lifetime*. Millerton, NY: Aperture, 1982.

Daniel, Pete, and Raymond Smock. *A Talent for Detail: The Photographs of Miss Frances Benjamin Johnston*. New York: Harmony Books, 1974.

Davis, Barbara A. *Edward S. Curtis: The Life and Times of a Shadow Catcher*. San Francisco: Chronicle Books, 1985.

DeWaard, E. John and Nancy DeWaard. *History of NASA: America's Voyage to the Stars*. New York: Simon & Schuster, 1985.

Hurley, F. Jack. *Marion Post Wolcott: A Photographic Journey*. Albuquerque: University of New Mexico Press, 1989.

Kunhardt, Dorothy Meserve, and Philip B. Kunhardt. *Mathew Brady and His World*. Alexandria, VA: Time-Life Books, 1977.

Newhall, Beaumont, and Howard Driggs. *William H. Jackson*. Dobbs Ferry, NY: Morgan and Morgan, 1974.

Plimpton, George. *Toni Frissell*. New York: Doubleday, 1994.

Rosenblum, Walter. *America and Lewis Hine: Photographs, 1904–1940*. Millerton, NY: Aperture, 1977.

Sandler, Martin W. *Photography: An Illustrated History*. New York: Oxford University Press, 2002.

Watson, Steven. *The Harlem Renaissance: Hub of African-American Culture*. New York: Pantheon, 1996.

PHOTO CREDITS

LEWIS HINE: *57, 65*, courtesy of George Eastman House; *58*, courtesy of the Naylor Collection; *59, 60, 63, 64, 69*, courtesy of the Library of Congress; *66*, courtesy of the photography collection, Miriam and Ira D. Wallach Division of Art, Prints and Photographs, the New York Public Library, Astor, Lenox and Tilden Foundations

EDWARD S. CURTIS: *71, 73*, courtesy of the Naylor Collection; *74, 77, 79, 81, 83*, courtesy of the Library of Congress; *78*, courtesy of Portland Art Museum, Portland, Oregon, gift of Dr. Fae Heath Batten

JAMES VAN DER ZEE: *85, 94, 97*, courtesy of the Naylor Collection; *87, 89, 90, 92, 93*, courtesy of the Library of Congress

DOROTHEA LANGE: *99, 102, 105, 106, 109, 110, 111, 113*, courtesy of the Library of Congress; *101*, courtesy of the Naylor Collection

MARION POST WOLCOTT: All photos courtesy of the Library of Congress

MARGARET BOURKE-WHITE: *129, 131, 138, 139, 140, 141*, courtesy of the Naylor Collection; *132*, courtesy of the St. Louis Art Museum; *135, 136*, courtesy of the Library of Congress

TONI FRISSELL: *143, 145, 147, 150, 155*, courtesy of the Library of Congress; *148, 152, 153*, courtesy of the National Archives

NASA AND NOAA: *157, 159, 160, 163, 164, 167*, courtesy of NASA; *168, 170, 171*, courtesy of NOAA

INDEX

(Page references in *italic* refer to illustrations.)

178